Original Title: 101 Strange But True Baseball Facts

© 101 Strange But True Baseball Facts, Carlos Martínez Cerdá and Víctor Martínez Cerdá, 2023

Authors: Víctor Martínez Cerdá and Carlos Martínez Cerdá (V&C Brothers)

© Cover and illustrations: V&C Brothers

Layout and design: V&C Brothers

101

STRANGE BUT TRUE
BASEBALL FACTS

INCREDIBLE AND
ASTONISHING EVENTS

1

**The exact origin of baseball is difficult to determine
due to its gradual evolution over time.**

Although there is no absolute consensus on when and where baseball
was invented, there is evidence that the game has its roots in ancient
bat-and-ball sports that were practiced in various cultures.

Prior to the misconception that Abner Doubleday invented baseball,
there are records indicating that similar games were played in different
parts of the world.

For example, a game called "rounders" was played in England since the
16th century, which had characteristics similar to modern baseball.

Other bat-and-ball games, such as "town ball" and "stool ball," were also
practiced in England.

In the United States, baseball began to gain popularity in the early 19th
century.

By the 1840s, the game had already established itself as an organized
sport with rules and teams in several cities across the United States.

Alexander Cartwright, a member of the New York Knickerbocker Base
Ball Club, is recognized for his contribution in creating the first formal
rules of modern baseball in 1845.

In 1907, a committee led by baseball historian A.G. Spalding conducted
an investigation to determine the origins of the game.

They concluded that baseball had developed gradually and could not be
attributed to a single invention or person.

Despite this, the story of Abner Doubleday as the supposed creator of
baseball continued to be ingrained in popular culture for a long time.

2

The New York Knickerbocker Club, also known as the New York Knickerbockers or Knickerbocker Base Ball Club, was an amateur baseball club established in New York City in 1845.

It was one of the earliest organized baseball clubs in the United States and played a pivotal role in standardizing the rules of the game.

The club was founded by a group of men, including Alexander Joy Cartwright, who is recognized as an important figure in the development of modern baseball.

Cartwright and other club members collaborated in creating a new set of rules for the game.

Among the rules established by the Knickerbockers was the use of an infield in the shape of a diamond, with bases placed at specific distances.

This configuration has become the standard in modern baseball.

Another key rule introduced by the Knickerbockers was the three strikes rule, which stated that a batter would be out if they failed to hit the ball after receiving three valid pitches.

This rule remains in baseball to this day.

The New York Knickerbocker Club played several matches in the following years, both against other clubs and among its own members.

Although the club did not exist for a long time, its influence on the history of baseball was significant, as it laid the groundwork for the rules and organization of the game.

3

The first recorded competitive baseball game took place on June 19, 1846, at the Elysian Fields in Hoboken, New Jersey.

This historic matchup was between the Knickerbockers and the New York Mutuals.

Led by Alexander Joy Cartwright, the Knickerbockers faced off against the New York Mutuals in a game that marked a milestone in baseball history.

However, the outcome was not favorable for the Knickerbockers, as they lost by an overwhelming score of 23 to 1 in just four innings.

It's important to note that this first game was not played under the exact rules used in modern baseball.

At that time, the rules were still in the process of development and evolution and had not been fully established.

Over time, the rules were adjusted and refined until they reached what we know today.

Despite the defeat in this first game, the Knickerbockers and other clubs of the era continued to play and perfect the sport.

Baseball grew increasingly popular and spread rapidly throughout the United States, becoming the national pastime of the country.

Since that historic game in 1846, baseball has grown tremendously in popularity and has become one of the most beloved and followed sports worldwide.

4

Baseball has had an intermittent relationship with the Olympic Games throughout history.

Although baseball debuted as an exhibition sport at the 1904 Summer Olympics in St. Louis, it did not become an official Olympic sport until 1992 when it was included in the program of the Barcelona Olympic Games.

From then on, baseball was contested as an Olympic sport at the Summer Games until 2008, held in Beijing.

At the 2004 Athens Olympics, Cuba won the gold medal in the baseball tournament.

However, after the 2008 Olympics, the International Olympic Committee (IOC) decided to remove baseball, along with softball, from the Olympic program.

This decision was made due to a combination of factors such as the lack of participation from major professional baseball leagues and the lack of globalization of the sport.

Fortunately, baseball has been revived and will be part of the Tokyo 2020 Olympics, which will be held in 2021 due to the COVID-19 pandemic.

In these Games, baseball will be present as an additional sport.

However, after Tokyo 2020, the future of baseball as an Olympic sport remains uncertain and will depend on the decisions of the IOC for future Olympic Games.

5

The Field of Dreams Game was a special event that paid tribute to the 1989 film "Field of Dreams."

A temporary stadium was built on the site where the movie was filmed, and the New York Yankees faced off against the Chicago White Sox in a regular-season Major League Baseball game.

The game was broadcasted by Fox and Fox Deportes and drew a significant audience of approximately 5,903,000 viewers, making it the most-watched baseball game in the past 16 years.

This particular game captured the attention of baseball fans due to the unique location and homage to the iconic movie.

The nostalgic atmosphere and the beauty of the temporary stadium built amidst the cornfields of Iowa contributed to making this a very special event.

6

**Baseball has a considerable global fan base,
estimated to be around 500 million people worldwide.**

However, it's important to note that the popularity of baseball varies in different regions, being more prominent in some countries compared to others.

The largest concentration of baseball fans is found in the United States, where the sport is considered one of the most popular and has a large fan base.

Baseball has a rich tradition in the United States, with Major League Baseball (MLB) being the top professional competition.

In addition to the United States, other Latin American countries such as Cuba and the Dominican Republic also have a significant fan base.

These countries have produced a great number of talented baseball players and have a strong baseball culture deeply rooted in their societies.

In terms of television viewership, baseball has been particularly popular in Japan.

The Nippon Professional Baseball (NPB), also known as the Japanese Baseball League, has attracted a large number of fans in the country and has generated substantial television rights deals.

It's important to highlight that viewership numbers and the popularity of baseball can change over time, and different sources may provide slightly different estimates.

However, overall, baseball remains a sport with a loyal and passionate fan base, especially in areas like the United States and certain countries in Latin America and Asia.

7

In 1903, the merger of two existing baseball leagues took place: the National League (NL), formed in 1876, and the American League (AL), established in 1901.

Prior to the merger, these two leagues operated as separate entities and competed against each other.

During that time, what became known as the "baseball war" occurred between the National League and the American League.

This rivalry was characterized by competition between the leagues to attract the best players and teams from the other league.

This was often achieved through the poaching of players from rival teams.

However, in 1903, the leagues decided to bury the hostilities and joined forces to form Major League Baseball (MLB) as a unified entity.

This led to the creation of the World Series, an annual event where the champions of the National League and the American League compete for the title of national baseball champion.

The World Series has become one of the premier events in the world of baseball and has helped solidify the popularity and importance of MLB as the leading professional baseball league in the United States and around the world.

8

The first World Series took place in 1903 and featured the Boston Americans (now known as the Boston Red Sox) from the American League and the Pittsburgh Pirates from the National League.

The series was played in a best-of-nine games format, rather than the current best-of-seven games format.

Boston secured victory by winning five games, while Pittsburgh won three.

The Boston Americans were crowned as the champions of the first World Series.

The 1903 World Series was a significant event in baseball history as it marked the beginning of an annual tradition where the champions of the two major leagues face off to determine the national champion.

Since then, the World Series has become one of the most prominent and highly anticipated sporting events in the world of baseball.

9

**Currently, Major League Baseball (MLB)
consists of a total of 30 teams.**

Of these teams, 29 are located in the United States and one in Canada.

Initially, each league, the American League (AL) and the National League (NL), had eight teams.

However, over the years, the number of teams has increased, and there has been significant expansion of the league.

During the 1960s, a major expansion took place that doubled the number of teams in MLB.

Then, in 1998, two more teams were added: the Arizona Diamondbacks and the Tampa Bay Devil Rays (now known as the Tampa Bay Rays), bringing the total number of teams to 30.

This configuration of 30 teams has remained since then, and each team competes in either the American League or the National League.

MLB teams participate in a regular season and compete for a spot in the playoffs, with the ultimate goal of reaching the World Series and becoming the Major League Baseball champion.

10

The record for the most wins in a 162-game season is 116 victories, achieved by two different teams in the history of Major League Baseball.

The first team to accomplish this feat was the Chicago Cubs in 1906.

During that season, the Cubs recorded a record of 116 wins and 36 losses, allowing them to dominate the National League and advance to the World Series.

However, they lost the World Series to the Chicago White Sox.

The second team to reach 116 wins in a season was the Seattle Mariners in 2001.

Under the leadership of manager Lou Piniella and with standout players like Ichiro Suzuki and Bret Boone, the Mariners achieved a record of 116 wins and 46 losses in the regular season.

Despite their success in the regular season, the Mariners were eliminated in the playoffs by the New York Yankees.

These two teams share the record for the most wins in a 162-game season in MLB.

It's important to note that the win record may change in the future as teams continue to compete in each new season.

11

Joe Nuxhall is known as the youngest player to appear in a Major League Baseball (MLB) game.

Nuxhall made his debut on June 10, 1944, with the Cincinnati Reds at the age of 15 years and 316 days.

As a left-handed pitcher, he became a curiosity in baseball history due to his youth.

On the other hand, Leroy "Satchel" Paige is famous for being the oldest player to participate in an MLB game.

Paige was a prominent pitcher in the Negro Leagues before getting the opportunity to play in the Major Leagues.

He made his MLB debut at the age of 42 on July 9, 1948, with the Cleveland Indians.

However, Paige continued to play in the minor leagues and independent leagues for many more years.

He played his last professional game at the age of nearly 60 in 1966.

Both Joe Nuxhall and Leroy "Satchel" Paige are iconic players in baseball history and have left a lasting legacy in the sport.

12

The longest baseball game in terms of time played in the history of Major League Baseball (MLB) lasted 8 hours and 6 minutes.

This game took place in May 1984 in Chicago and pitted the Chicago White Sox against the Milwaukee Brewers.

The game extended over 25 innings spanning two days, and the White Sox ultimately won with a score of 7-6.

As for the fastest game in MLB history, it occurred on September 28, 1919, between the New York Giants and the Philadelphia Phillies.

This game lasted only 51 minutes, setting a record as the fastest recorded baseball game.

The New York Giants won the game with a score of 6-1.

These two games represent opposite extremes in terms of the duration of a baseball game, showcasing the variability and exciting nature of the sport throughout its history.

13

**Each baseball used in Major League Baseball (MLB)
is composed of a rubber or cork core covered
with horsehide or white cowhide.**

These balls are hand-stitched with 108 double red
stitches.

The first and last stitches are hidden behind the
leather to ensure a smooth surface.

As for the lifespan of a baseball in MLB, it varies
depending on the game and circumstances.

It is estimated that a baseball has an average lifespan
of about seven pitches before being taken out of play.

During a game, between 6 and 10 dozen balls are used
as they are constantly replaced due to wear, damage,
or a loss of performance.

The quality and consistency of baseballs are of utmost
importance in the game, and MLB has strict standards
to ensure that all balls meet the required
specifications.

This includes the size, weight, compression, and the
precise stitches mentioned above.

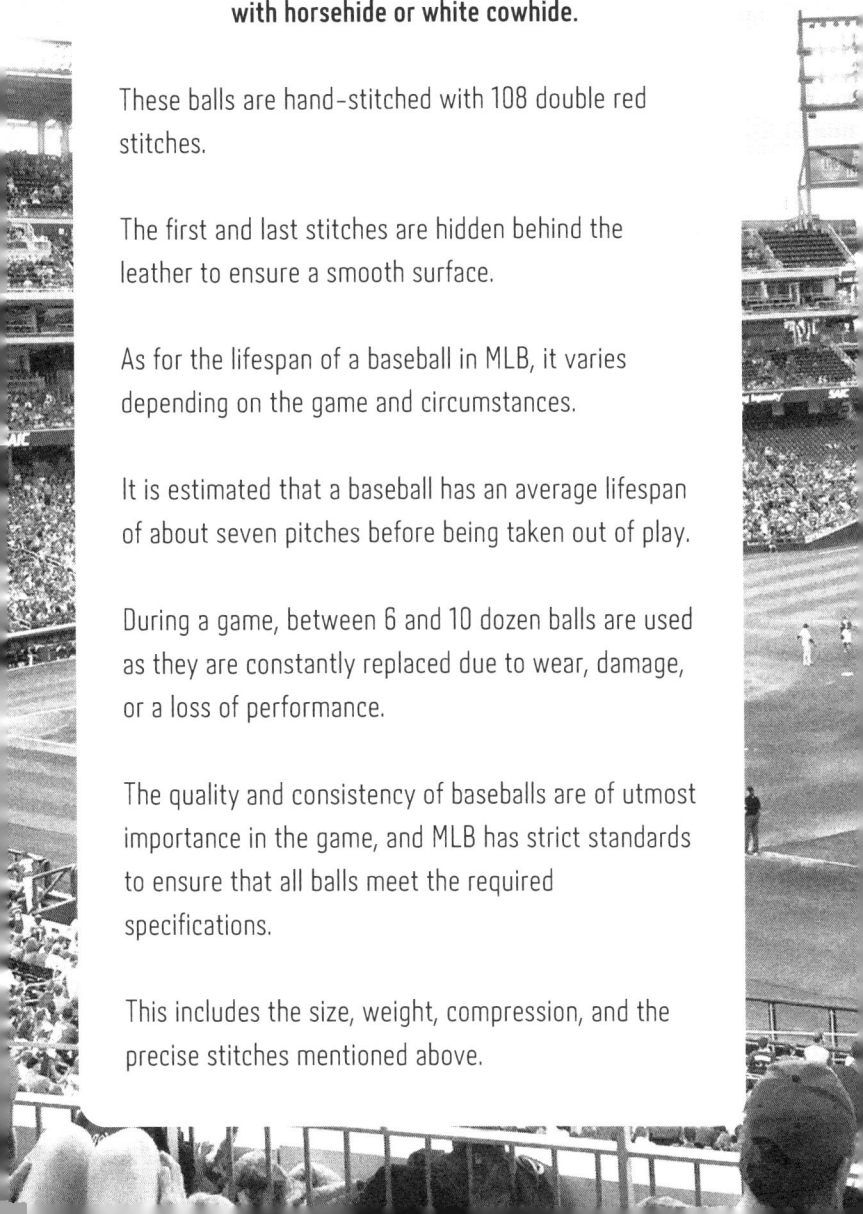

14

For much of the 20th century, African Americans were excluded from competing in Major League Baseball (MLB) due to the prevailing racial segregation policy in the United States.

This policy, known as the "color line," prohibited Black players from being part of Major League teams.

In the face of this discrimination, the so-called "Negro Leagues" were formed where African American players competed against each other.

These leagues, such as the Negro League and the Negro National League, featured some of the finest baseball talents and became a showcase for Black players.

However, in 1947, the barrier of racial segregation was finally broken when Jackie Robinson signed a contract with the MLB's Brooklyn Dodgers.

Robinson became the first African American player to play in the Major Leagues in the modern era.

His historic debut on April 15, 1947, marked a significant milestone in baseball history and in the struggle for racial equality in sports and society at large.

Jackie Robinson's contribution paved the way for other African American players to enter MLB, and since then, baseball has become a more inclusive and diverse sport.

Jackie Robinson is widely recognized and celebrated for his courage and talent, and his jersey number, 42, was retired across all MLB teams as a tribute to his impact and legacy in the sport.

15

Aroldis Chapman, who has played for several teams in MLB, is known for his incredible velocity in his pitches.

On September 24, 2010, while playing for the Cincinnati Reds, Chapman threw a fastball recorded at a speed of 105.1 mph (169.1 km/h).

This was the highest recorded speed for a pitch in the history of Major League Baseball at that time.

Chapman continued to showcase his power in the following years.

On September 18, 2011, pitching for the Reds against the San Diego Padres, he recorded a pitch at 105 mph (168.9 km/h).

Then, on September 24, 2016, while playing for the Chicago Cubs against the St. Louis Cardinals, he threw another pitch at 105 mph (168.9 km/h).

These pitches rank among the fastest in baseball history.

It is important to note that pitch velocities can vary depending on different factors, such as the measurement technology used and the game conditions.

However, Chapman's pitches have been recognized as some of the fastest and most powerful in the history of professional baseball.

16

The oldest baseball stadium still in use today is Fenway Park, located in Boston, Massachusetts.

It was inaugurated on April 20, 1912 and is the home of the Boston Red Sox of Major League Baseball (MLB).

Fenway Park is known for its rich history and unique architecture.

It has witnessed numerous iconic baseball moments and has hosted 11 World Series games, including the famous "Red Sox Miracle" in 2004 when the team ended an 86-year championship drought.

Over the years, some renovations have been made to Fenway Park to modernize it and improve the facilities, but the stadium has maintained its charm and historic features, such as the famous Green Monster, an 11.3-meter-high wall in left field.

Fenway Park is considered an icon of baseball and a popular tourist destination for sports fans.

Its longevity and the passion of the fans who fill its seats make Fenway Park a special place in baseball history.

17

Baseball, specifically Major League Baseball (MLB), generates significant revenue.

The total revenues of the MLB vary from year to year, but in 2020, it was estimated to surpass $3.5 billion.

It is important to note that these numbers can be affected by factors such as the COVID-19 pandemic, which negatively impacted the season and associated revenues.

The average revenue per team in MLB in 2020 was around $122 million.

However, it is important to highlight that revenues can vary significantly between teams, as factors like location, market size, and team performance can influence revenue generation.

MLB has experienced steady growth in its revenues in recent decades.

Compared to 2010, it is estimated that league revenues have doubled.

Furthermore, it is expected that MLB revenues will surpass $11 billion in 2022.

Television broadcasting contracts play a significant role in MLB's revenue generation.

The league has signed broadcasting deals with various television networks and streaming platforms such as ESPN, Turner Sports, and Apple, providing them with an additional source of revenue.

18

The New York Yankees are widely recognized as the most valuable franchise in MLB and in all of baseball.

According to the latest estimates, the value of the Yankees exceeds $5 billion.

This figure is based on several factors such as the team's successful history, large fan base, and their position in one of the largest and wealthiest markets in the United States.

The Yankees have had remarkable success throughout their history, winning the World Series numerous times.

They have won the World Series championship 27 times, making them the most successful team in the history of Major League Baseball.

Their on-field success and their identity as one of the most iconic franchises in the sport have contributed to their value and commercial appeal.

In addition to their sporting success, the Yankees have built a strong and recognizable brand worldwide.

Their iconic logo and their rich history of baseball stars have helped establish them as one of the most recognized and valuable sports brands worldwide.

19

Throughout the history of baseball, the size of bats has evolved and has been subject to regulations by leagues and governing bodies of the sport.

Currently, MLB regulations establish certain dimensions for bats to be considered legal.

Below, we provide information on the current dimensions of bats in MLB, as well as some historical data:

-Length: Currently, there is no maximum length established for MLB bats. However, most players use bats ranging from 32 to 34 inches in length. Some players may prefer shorter bats for better control, while others may opt for longer bats for increased reach.

-Diameter: The maximum diameter allowed for an MLB bat is 2.61 inches. This measurement refers to the thickness of the bat barrel at its widest point. Players have some flexibility to choose the diameter that feels most comfortable and effective for them.

It is important to note that while there are regulations on the dimensions of bats in MLB, players may have individual preferences and can customize their bats within the established limits.

Some players may choose lighter or heavier bats, or may have additional specifications to suit their playing style.

Furthermore, throughout history, there have been changes in the regulations and standards of bats.

20

The materials used in bats by MLB players can vary, and there is no exact figure indicating the precise percentage of players using maple wood bats.

However, it is true that the use of maple bats has become increasingly popular in recent years.

–Use of maple wood bats: Starting in the 2000s, the use of maple wood bats in MLB has increased significantly. Many players have chosen to use maple bats due to their higher density and hardness compared to ash bats. It is believed that maple bats can provide greater power and durability, which has led to an increase in their popularity.

–Influence of Barry Bonds: Barry Bonds' standout season in 2001, in which he set the record of 73 home runs, played a significant role in popularizing maple bats. Bonds used a maple bat during that season, and his success inspired other players to try this material and adopt it in their own games.

–Aluminum bats: While aluminum bats are popular at lower levels of baseball, such as high school, college, and minor leagues, they are not allowed in MLB. In MLB, players must use wood bats or composite bats approved by the league. Aluminum bats are usually lighter and more durable than wood bats, but they are not used at the professional level.

21

The introduction of metal bats in baseball:

–First patent: In 1924, William Shroyer received a patent for a design of a metal bat. However, at that time, metal bats were not widely used in baseball.

–Introduction of aluminum bat: In the 1970s, the Worth Sports Company developed and introduced the first aluminum baseball bat. This new type of bat offered some advantages in terms of durability and weight compared to traditional wooden bats.

–Popularization of aluminum bats: After their introduction, aluminum bats quickly gained popularity. Worth Sports Company soon became one of the leading manufacturers of aluminum bats in the United States.

–Use in youth and college leagues: In 1974, Worth produced the first official aluminum bats for Little League and NCAA college leagues. This allowed younger players and college students to experiment with aluminum bats in their competitions.

Since then, aluminum bats have been widely used in lower levels of baseball, such as youth leagues and colleges.

However, in Major League Baseball (MLB), wooden bats and league-approved composite bats remain the only ones allowed in professional competition.

22

Corked baseball bats.

-**Lightness and speed**: By corking a baseball bat or using other less dense materials, the weight of the bat can be reduced, theoretically allowing for a faster swing. It is believed that a faster swing could generate greater ball speed upon contact, which in turn could result in increased hitting distance.

-**Weakening of the bat**: However, cork and other lighter materials are not as strong as wood, which weakens the structure of the bat. This means that corked bats are more likely to suffer damage or break during the game, especially when the ball is hit with significant force.

-**Illegality in MLB**: The use of corked bats is strictly prohibited in Major League Baseball (MLB). League rules state that bats must be made entirely of wood and cannot have any alterations that attempt to enhance performance. If a player is found using a corked bat during an MLB game, they may face penalties, including disciplinary actions and possibly expulsion from the league.

The belief that corked baseball bats increase hitting distance is widely considered a myth.

Numerous studies and tests have shown that cork does not provide a significant advantage in terms of hitting distance.

Instead, performance in baseball relies more on the batter's technique and other factors such as physical strength and coordination.

23

The Louisville Slugger brand is one of the most recognized and popular in the baseball bat industry.

-Origins: The history of Louisville Slugger began in 1884 when young Bud Hillerich, a carpenter's apprentice in Louisville, Kentucky, made his first baseball bat. The first player to use it was Pete Browning, who had broken his own bat during a game. Browning was impressed with Hillerich's bat and spread the word among other players, leading to a growing demand for the handmade bats by Hillerich.

-Growth and expansion: As the popularity of Hillerich's bats increased, the company started to grow and expand. In 1894, the company officially adopted the name "Hillerich & Bradsby Co." and established its factory in Louisville. Over the years, the company has continued to innovate and improve its products, using different types of wood and manufacturing techniques to produce high-quality bats.

-Industry icon: Louisville Slugger has become a true icon in the baseball industry. Its bats have been used by numerous famous players throughout baseball history, including Babe Ruth, Ted Williams, and Hank Aaron. The distinctive Louisville Slugger logo, featuring an image of a batter in a hitting position, has become a recognized symbol in the world of baseball.

-Current popularity: Today, Louisville Slugger remains one of the most popular and widely used brands in baseball. It is estimated that around 20% of Major League Baseball (MLB) players use Louisville Slugger bats. The company continues to produce a wide variety of bat models to suit the preferences and needs of players.

24

Babe Ruth, whose real name was George Herman Ruth Jr., is considered one of the greatest baseball players of all time.

Although he is most known for his batting ability, he also began his career as a pitcher.

-Debut as a pitcher: Babe Ruth made his Major League debut on July 11, 1914, as a pitcher for the Boston Red Sox. In his first season, he had a record of 2-1 with a 3.91 ERA in 5 games.

-Success as a pitcher: During his early seasons, Ruth proved to be a talented pitcher and achieved great success. In 1916, he led the American League in ERA with 1.75 and had a record of 23 wins and 12 losses. The following year, he had a record of 24-13 with a 2.01 ERA.

-Transition to a batter role: As Ruth developed his batting skill, his value as a pitcher began to diminish. The Red Sox decided to use him more frequently as an outfielder and hitter, capitalizing on his powerful swing.

-Move to the New York Yankees: In 1920, the Boston Red Sox sold Ruth to the New York Yankees, which turned out to be a historic moment that changed the dynamics of baseball. Ruth became the star player of the Yankees and contributed to their success in the following decades.

-Records as a batter: Babe Ruth is widely known for his batting ability. He set numerous offensive records during his career, including the single-season home run record (60 in 1927) and the lifetime home run record (714 until it was surpassed by Hank Aaron in 1974).

-Success with the Yankees: With the Yankees, Ruth won seven American League pennants and four World Series. His presence on the team helped turn the Yankees into a legendary franchise and established the Yankees' dynasty in the 1920s and 1930s.

-Legacy and recognition: Babe Ruth is considered an icon of baseball and one of the most important athletes in the history of the United States. He was inducted into the Baseball Hall of Fame in 1936 as one of its inaugural members. Although he began his career as a pitcher, it was his impact as a batter and his ability to hit home runs that catapulted him to fame and allowed him to leave a lasting legacy in the world of baseball.

25

Barry Bonds is the baseball player with the most Most Valuable Player (MVP) awards in Major League Baseball (MLB).

-MVP Awards: Barry Bonds has received a total of seven National League MVP awards. He won these awards in the seasons of 1990, 1992, 1993, 2001, 2002, 2003, and 2004. He is the player with the most MVPs in MLB history.

-All-time home run record: Barry Bonds also holds the record for the most home runs in a career in MLB history, with a total of 762 home runs. He surpassed the previous record of Hank Aaron (755) on August 7, 2007.

-Single-season home run record: In the 2001 season, Barry Bonds set the record for the most home runs in a single season by hitting 73 home runs. This record surpassed the previous mark of 70 home runs set by Mark McGwire in 1998.

-Walks record: Bonds also holds the record for the most career walks in MLB, with a total of 2,558 walks received. This record showcases his ability to be patient at the plate and his knack for avoiding difficult pitches.

However, despite his impressive on-field achievements, Barry Bonds has been surrounded by controversy due to his association with steroid use and doping in baseball.

Scandals and accusations have affected his reputation and have led to his exclusion from the Baseball Hall of Fame thus far.

Although he has been eligible for induction into the Hall of Fame, he has not garnered the necessary votes from the members of the Baseball Writers' Association of America (BBWAA) to be included.

26

Mike Trout is one of the best baseball players currently and has made a significant impact on the sport.

-Professional career: Mike Trout was selected in the first round of the MLB draft in 2009 by the Los Angeles Angels. He made his debut in the Major Leagues in 2011 and has since been a dominant force in baseball.

-Skills and statistics: Trout is known for his complete game and impact in all facets of the game. He is an excellent hitter with a powerful swing and a great ability to get on base. Additionally, he is a fast runner and an outstanding defender in center field.

-Achievements and recognition: Throughout his career, Trout has accumulated numerous achievements and recognition. He has been selected to the All-Star Game multiple times and has won several Most Valuable Player (MVP) awards in the American League. As of my knowledge cutoff date in September 2021, he had won three MVP awards in the seasons 2014, 2016, and 2019.

-Impressive statistics: Trout has had impressive seasons in terms of statistics. In addition to the mentioned record of hitting 30 home runs, stealing 45 bases, and scoring 125 runs in a single season, he has led the league in various categories such as on-base percentage (OBP) and walks received.

-Acknowledgment of his talent: Trout is widely regarded as one of the best young players in baseball history. His ability to consistently produce at the plate, his speed on the bases, and his defensive prowess have led him to be acclaimed as one of the premier players in the current game.

27

Ted Williams is widely regarded as one of the greatest hitters in baseball history and has been acclaimed as the "greatest hitter who ever lived."

-Professional career: Ted Williams played in the Major Leagues for 19 seasons, all with the Boston Red Sox, from 1939 to 1960. During that time, he became one of the most iconic figures in the franchise.

-Hitting ability: Williams was known for his exceptional hitting ability. He had a refined batting technique and keen eyesight that allowed him to accurately identify pitches. His plate discipline and ability to recognize balls and strikes helped him achieve excellent offensive results.

-.400 batting average: In the 1941 season, Ted Williams accomplished a historic feat by finishing with a .406 batting average. He was the last player in MLB to achieve a batting average over .400 in a full season. This achievement is considered one of the most remarkable accomplishments in baseball history.

-Power and productivity: In addition to his ability to hit for a high average, Williams also displayed great power at the plate. He ended his career with 521 home runs and 1,839 runs batted in. He also led the American League in home runs four times and in RBIs twice.

-Other notable statistics: In addition to his batting average and power, Williams was also known for his ability to get on base and draw walks. He finished his career with an on-base percentage of .482, the highest in Major League history at that time.

-Honors and recognition: Ted Williams was selected to the All-Star Game 19 times, won two American League MVP awards, and received the American League Batting Champion title six times. He was also inducted into the Baseball Hall of Fame in 1966, in his first year of eligibility.

Ted Williams left a lasting legacy in baseball with his exceptional hitting ability and meticulous approach to the art of batting.

His impact on the sport and his reputation as one of the greatest hitters of all time have secured him a prominent place in baseball history.

28

Hank Aaron, also known as "Hammerin' Hank," was an outstanding baseball player who left a lasting legacy in the sport.

-Home run record: On April 8, 1974, Hank Aaron became the player to break Babe Ruth's home run record by hitting his 715th home run in a game against the Los Angeles Dodgers. Ultimately, Aaron finished his career with a total of 755 home runs, a record that stood until it was surpassed by Barry Bonds in 2007.

-Consistency in home run production: Aaron demonstrated remarkable consistency in home run production throughout his career. He hit at least 30 home runs in a single season on fifteen occasions, a record he shares with the legendary Babe Ruth. His ability to generate power consistently made him one of the most feared hitters of his time.

-All-Star selections record: Hank Aaron was selected to the All-Star Game a total of 25 times, a record that still stands. His ability to maintain a high level of performance and his popularity among fans led to consistent selection to the All-Star team.

-All-Star games played record: Aaron also shares the record for most All-Star games played, having participated in 24 All-Star games throughout his career. He shares this record with the legendary Willie Mays and Stan Musial.

-Other achievements and recognition: In addition to his records and All-Star selections, Hank Aaron was named the National League Most Valuable Player (MVP) in 1957 and won three batting titles in his career. He was also inducted into the Baseball Hall of Fame in 1982, in his first year of eligibility.

Hank Aaron left an indelible mark on baseball and is considered one of the greatest players in the history of the sport.

His consistency in home run production, batting ability, and All-Star selection record established him as an iconic figure in the game.

29

The player who holds the record for the most career grand slams in baseball is Alex Rodriguez, commonly known as A-Rod.

-Grand slam record: Alex Rodriguez hit a total of 25 grand slams in his Major League career. A grand slam is a type of home run that occurs when a player hits a home run with the bases loaded, thereby scoring four runs for their team with a single hit.

-500 home run milestone: Rodriguez became the youngest player to reach 500 home runs in his MLB career. He achieved this feat at the age of 32 years and 8 days on August 4, 2007. In total, he finished his career with 696 home runs, placing him fourth on the all-time list as of my knowledge cutoff in September 2021.

-Lucrative contracts: Alex Rodriguez has been recognized not only for his on-field achievements but also for the multimillion-dollar contracts he has signed in his career. In 2001, he signed a 10-year contract with the Texas Rangers worth $252 million, at that time the largest contract in the history of the sport. Then, in 2007, he signed another historic contract with the New York Yankees for 10 years and $275 million, surpassing his own record.

30

Ty Cobb, known as "The Georgia Peach," is considered one of the greatest baseball players of all time.

–Batting average: Ty Cobb holds the record for the highest career batting average with an average of .366. During his 24 years in the Major Leagues, primarily playing for the Detroit Tigers, Cobb displayed incredible consistency in his ability to connect hits and get on base.

–Batting titles: Cobb also holds the record for the most career batting titles won with a total of 12. He won his first title in 1907 and his last in 1919. His ability to maintain a high batting average throughout his career distinguishes him as one of the greatest hitters in baseball history.

–Additional statistics and achievements: In addition to his impressive batting average and batting titles, Cobb accumulated numerous standout statistics. He finished his career with 4,189 hits, a record that stood for many years. He also led the league in runs scored eight times and stolen bases six times.

–Inclusion in the Hall of Fame: Ty Cobb was one of the earliest players to be inducted into the Baseball Hall of Fame in 1936. His influence on the game and his batting dominance secured him a prominent place in baseball history.

Ty Cobb left a lasting legacy in baseball with his exceptional batting ability and aggressiveness in the game.

His batting average record and mastery in the batter's box establish him as one of the greatest hitters of all time.

31

The player with the most career victories in MLB is Cy Young, whose real name was Denton True Young.

-Win record: Cy Young recorded a total of 511 victories in his Major League career. It is the highest record in baseball history and is considered one of the most impressive accomplishments in the sport.

-Loss record: Along with his win record, Young also holds the record for the most career losses with a total of 315. This is partly due to his longevity as a pitcher, as he played for 22 seasons.

-Innings pitched record: Young also holds the record for the most innings pitched in his career, accumulating a total of 7,356 innings. This record demonstrates his endurance and ability to stay in the game for long periods of time.

-Games started record: Additionally, Cy Young holds the record for the most games started in his career with a total of 815 starts. This reflects his role as a dominant and reliable pitcher in his era.

-Cy Young Award: After his death in 1955, the Cy Young Award was established in his honor. This award is given annually to the best pitcher in each league in Major League Baseball. It is a way to recognize his impact and legacy in the sport.

32

"A League of Their Own" is a baseball film that was released in 1992.

-Synopsis: A League of Their Own tells the fictional story of the All-American Girls Professional Baseball League, a women's baseball league established during World War II when many male players were serving in the military. The film focuses on two sisters, Dottie and Kit, who join the Rockford Peaches, a women's baseball team, and their journey in the world of professional baseball.

-Cast: The film features a notable cast, including Geena Davis as Dottie Hinson, Tom Hanks as Jimmy Dugan (the team's coach), Madonna, Rosie O'Donnell, and Lori Petty, among other actors.

-Directing and production: A League of Their Own was directed by Penny Marshall and produced by Elliot Abbott and Robert Greenhut. The film was well-received by both critics and audiences and became a box office success.

-Box office and commercial success: A League of Their Own was a major box office success. According to reports, the film grossed $107.5 million worldwide, making it the highest-grossing baseball film of all time as of my knowledge cutoff in September 2021.

The film received positive reviews for its performances, direction, and unique theme of women's baseball during a specific historical period.

A League of Their Own has become a sports film classic and has left a lasting impact on popular culture.

33

Baseballs are rubbed with a very specific type of mud before each game.

This process of rubbing the balls with mud is done to enhance the grip of the ball and make it more manageable during the game.

The mud used comes from the New Jersey side of the Delaware River, specifically from an area known as Lena Blackburne Original Baseball Rubbing Mud.

Lena Blackburne's mud has been used in professional baseball since the 1930s.

Lena Blackburne, a former player and coach, accidentally discovered the power of the mud while searching for a way to condition new balls so they wouldn't be too slippery.

After trying various materials, he found a special mud on the banks of the Delaware River that served his purpose.

Lena Blackburne's mud is hand-collected and carefully cleaned to remove any impurities.

It is then mixed with water to achieve a suitable consistency for rubbing the balls.

This process of rubbing the balls with the mud is carried out before every professional baseball game to prepare the balls and give them the proper grip.

Rubbing the balls with Lena Blackburne's mud helps remove the shine and dirt from new balls, allowing pitchers to have better control and infield players to have a better grip when catching and throwing the ball.

Additionally, the mud also contributes to smoothing the surface of the ball and reducing the unpredictable bounce that could occur with a new and shiny ball.

It is important to note that the use of this mud is a unique tradition in baseball and is considered part of the game.

It has become a standard practice in Major League Baseball (MLB) and other levels of the sport.

Lena Blackburne's mud is widely recognized and used throughout professional baseball to prepare the balls before each game.

34

"Take Me Out to the Ball Game" is considered the unofficial anthem of American baseball.

It was written by Jack Norworth and Albert Von Tilzer in 1908, and it has become one of the most recognized and popular songs associated with the sport.

The song tells the story of a person longing to attend a baseball game and enjoy the experience at the stadium.

Although the original lyrics do not mention a woman, a version that included Katie Casey, a passionate baseball fan, became popular.

The chorus of the song is the most recognizable part and is traditionally sung during the seventh-inning stretch at every baseball game.

The seventh inning is considered a special moment in the game, and the tradition of singing this song during that time has become ingrained in American baseball culture.

Although "Take Me Out to the Ball Game" has become an iconic baseball song in the United States, it is important to note that it is not the official anthem of the sport.

The national anthem of the United States, "The Star-Spangled Banner," is performed before many baseball games as part of the tradition and respect for the country.

"Take Me Out to the Ball Game" has been performed and covered by numerous artists over the years, and its catchy melody and optimistic lyrics make it a beloved song among baseball fans.

It is an integral part of the stadium experience and has become a symbol of the passion and tradition of the sport.

35

William Howard Taft.

He was the first president to throw a ceremonial pitch at a baseball game.

Taft, who was a baseball fan and had played semi-professionally, threw the first ceremonial pitch on April 14, 1910, at a game between the Washington Senators and the Philadelphia Athletics in Washington, D.C.

Taft's pitch established a tradition that has endured over the years.

Since then, most U.S. presidents have thrown the first pitch on Opening Day of the baseball season.

However, there are some notable exceptions.

Jimmy Carter, Donald Trump, and Joe Biden did not throw the first ceremonial pitch during their presidencies.

Although there is no specific reason why they did not participate in this tradition, each president has the option to decide whether they want to throw the pitch or not.

The ceremonial first pitch by the president is a symbolic and festive moment in American baseball.

It is considered an honor for the president and also adds excitement and celebration to the start of the professional baseball season.

36

The Black Sox scandal, also known as the "Black Sox Scandal," was one of the most shocking and notorious moments in baseball history.

It occurred in 1919 and continues to be a subject of debate and fascination among historians and sports fans.

In that year, eight players from the Chicago White Sox, one of the most successful teams of the time, were accused of conspiring to intentionally throw the World Series against the Cincinnati Reds in exchange for money from a gambling syndicate.

The players involved were Eddie Cicotte, Chick Gandil, Happy Felsch, Shoeless Joe Jackson, Fred McMullin, Swede Risberg, Buck Weaver, and Claude "Lefty" Williams.

The scandal rocked baseball and the nation as a whole.

It was hard for fans and the general public to believe that professional players could betray the game in such a way.

The case received significant media attention and became a topic of national discussion.

Although the players were acquitted of the charges in the 1920 trial, Commissioner Kenesaw Mountain Landis took a firm stance and permanently banned them from organized baseball.

Landis's decision sent a clear message that dishonest behavior and game-fixing would not be tolerated in the sport.

The Black Sox scandal had a profound impact on baseball.

It led to major reforms in the structure and regulation of the game, including the creation of the commissioner's position and stricter measures against illegal gambling and corruption in the sport.

It also left a stain on the reputation of some players and taught a lasting lesson about the importance of integrity and honesty in baseball and sports in general.

37

**Ken Griffey Sr. and Ken Griffey Jr. were the first father-son duo to play
in Major League Baseball (MLB) at the same time and for the
same team, the Seattle Mariners.**

Ken Griffey Sr., born on April 10, 1950, was an outstanding outfielder and hitter in MLB during his 19-year career.

He played for various teams throughout his career but is best known for his years with the Cincinnati Reds, where he was part of the World Series-winning team in 1975 and 1976.

Griffey Sr. was a standout hitter and a versatile player in the field.

Ken Griffey Jr., born on November 21, 1969, is widely regarded as one of the greatest baseball players of all time.

He was a talented center fielder and a powerful hitter, known for his graceful playing style and ability to make spectacular catches in center field.

Griffey Jr. spent the majority of his career with the Seattle Mariners and also had brief stints with the Cincinnati Reds and the Chicago White Sox.

In 1990, Ken Griffey Jr. made his MLB debut with the Seattle Mariners, while his father, Ken Griffey Sr., was on the team as an outfielder and designated hitter.

Playing together on the same team at the same time was a historic and exciting event for baseball.

Both players had a significant impact on the Mariners and left their mark on the sport.

Ken Griffey Jr.'s career was particularly notable as he was elected to the Baseball Hall of Fame in 2016 in his first year of eligibility.

His father, Ken Griffey Sr., is also remembered as a talented and respected player in baseball history.

The combination of Ken Griffey Sr. and Ken Griffey Jr. as the first father-son duo to play in MLB at the same time and for the same team is a significant milestone in baseball history.

Their legacy continues to be recognized and appreciated by baseball fans to this day.

38

In the past, visiting teams in baseball used to wear gray uniforms.

This custom dates back to the early days of organized baseball in the 19th century.

However, it is important to note that rules and conventions regarding uniforms have evolved over time and may vary today.

In the early years of baseball, visiting teams often struggled to wash their uniforms while traveling.

This was due to time limitations and limited access to proper laundry facilities.

As a result, they opted to wear gray uniforms, which were more effective at hiding dirt and stains that inevitably accumulated during their travels.

On the other hand, home teams typically wore white because it was easier to wash and keep clean.

Additionally, white uniforms allowed the local players to stand out better on the field and be more easily identifiable to umpires and spectators.

With the passage of time and the development of the sport, visiting teams no longer face the same logistical limitations regarding the washing of their uniforms.

Furthermore, rules and conventions regarding uniforms have evolved.

Nowadays, visiting teams can wear a variety of colors and are not limited to gray.

39

**Babe Ruth baseball cards are some of the most
valuable and sought-after by collectors.**

Babe Ruth is considered one of the most iconic figures in baseball
history, and his cards are highly coveted due to their historical
significance and his legacy in the sport.

Recently, in January 2021, it was reported that a baseball card
depicting Babe Ruth as a minor league pitcher for the Baltimore
Orioles was sold to a private buyer.

This particular card, known as Babe Ruth's 1914 "RMY" card, is
extremely rare and valuable.

The exact sale price was not disclosed, but it was estimated to be
worth around £4.3 million, making it the most valuable baseball
card ever sold.

The rarity and condition of baseball cards are key factors that
influence their value.

In the case of Babe Ruth cards, their historical significance and
popularity as one of the most legendary players of all time also
play a significant role in their demand and price in the collector's
market.

It is important to note that the baseball card market is dynamic,
and prices can change over time.

Other Babe Ruth cards, as well as cards of other historic and
renowned players, have also reached significant prices in auctions
and private sales.

The demand and value of rare and valuable baseball cards are
influenced by various factors, including scarcity, condition, age,
and the historical importance of the player depicted.

40

Hitting four home runs in a single game is undoubtedly considered one of the greatest achievements in the history of baseball.

Accomplishing this feat demonstrates exceptional power-hitting ability and consistency.

As of my knowledge cutoff in September 2021, a total of 18 players have achieved this remarkable milestone in Major League Baseball (MLB).

The first player to accomplish it was Bobby Lowe on May 30, 1894.

In that game, Lowe hit four home runs for the Boston Beaneaters.

Since then, other players have achieved this notable feat, including prominent names such as Lou Gehrig, Willie Mays, Mike Schmidt, Mark Whiten, and Shawn Green, among others.

The most recent player to hit four home runs in a single game was JD Martinez, who accomplished it on September 4, 2017, as a member of the Arizona Diamondbacks.

This achievement is considered extremely rare and difficult to attain due to the combination of skill, opportunity, and exceptional performance in a single game.

Hitting a home run in a game is already an impressive feat, so hitting four in a single game demonstrates an extraordinary display of power and prowess at the plate.

Throughout the history of baseball, there have been exciting and memorable moments when a player achieves the feat of hitting four home runs in a single game.

These exceptional performances are remembered and celebrated by baseball fans and stand out as notable milestones in the history of the sport.

41

The most expensive autographed baseball in history was sold for the astonishing sum of $191,200.

The auction took place on May 5, 2006, in Dallas, Texas, and was organized by Heritage Auction Galleries.

The baseball was autographed by Joe DiMaggio, a baseball legend.

Joe DiMaggio was an American professional baseball player who served as a center fielder for the New York Yankees from 1936 to 1951.

He is widely recognized as one of the greatest players in baseball history and is considered one of the greatest hitters of all time.

During his career, DiMaggio achieved numerous accomplishments and records.

He was a nine-time All-Star player and won the Most Valuable Player Award in the American League three times.

Additionally, he set the incredible record of hitting safely in 56 consecutive games during the 1941 season, a record that still stands today.

The sale of the baseball autographed by Joe DiMaggio for $191,200 reflects his status as a baseball legend and the high demand for items related to him.

Auctions of autographed sports memorabilia are common, especially when it comes to iconic figures like DiMaggio.

42

There was a historic event in baseball involving Lou Gehrig and Babe Ruth, two prominent players of the 1930s.

Both were struck out by a 17-year-old pitcher named Jackie Mitchell while playing for a minor league team.

Lou Gehrig was a famous American baseball player who served as a first baseman for the New York Yankees from 1923 to 1939.

He is considered one of the greatest players in baseball history and is known for his durability and power as a hitter.

Gehrig was nicknamed "The Iron Horse" and set numerous records during his career, including the consecutive games played record that stood for over 50 years.

Babe Ruth, on the other hand, also played for the New York Yankees for a large part of his career, from 1920 to 1934.

Ruth is widely recognized as one of the greatest hitters in baseball history and is considered one of the most important sports icons of all time.

His batting skills and home run power made him a legendary figure.

The aforementioned Jackie Mitchell gained notoriety in 1931 when she was signed by the Chattanooga Lookouts, a minor league team in Tennessee.

During an exhibition game against the New York Yankees, Mitchell managed to strike out both star players, Lou Gehrig and Babe Ruth, which caught the attention of the media and baseball fans.

This event became a headline story in the newspapers of the time and created a stir in the baseball community.

However, some reports suggest that the event may have been a publicity stunt.

Babe Ruth, known for his flamboyant personality, possibly collaborated with the performance by allowing himself to be struck out to generate publicity and increase interest in the exhibition game.

While it cannot be confirmed with certainty, this theory suggests that Mitchell's strikeouts of Ruth and Gehrig may have been a planned maneuver.

43

Hot dogs are undoubtedly one of the most popular foods in baseball stadiums.

They are considered an iconic part of the baseball experience, and it is common for fans to enjoy them during games.

It is estimated that over 26 million hot dogs and sausages are consumed in stadiums during a typical baseball season.

The association between hot dogs and baseball has an interesting history.

The tradition of eating hot dogs at baseball games dates back to European immigrants who arrived in the United States in the 19th and 20th centuries.

Specifically, it is believed to have been influenced by German immigrants who introduced Frankfurt-style sausages to the United States.

These sausages were easy to make and handle, and street vendors began offering them at baseball stadiums due to their convenience and popularity.

The bond between hot dogs and baseball has strengthened over time, becoming an entrenched tradition in the sports culture.

Fans associate the experience of enjoying a hot dog while watching a baseball game as an essential part of their stadium visit.

It is important to note that the popularity of hot dogs in baseball stadiums is not limited to the United States alone but extends to other countries where baseball is a significant sport.

44

The New York Yankees are pioneers in introducing numbers on the back of baseball uniforms.

Although it had been attempted earlier in 1916, it was deemed "improper" at that time, even if they were located on the uniform sleeves.

However, when the Yankees proposed the idea, all teams decided to follow their example.

This change occurred at a time when the Yankees had won two consecutive World Series titles and had prominent players like Babe Ruth and Lou Gehrig on their team.

Their success and popularity influenced the acceptance of the innovation of numbers on uniforms by other baseball teams.

The introduction of numbers on uniforms allowed for easier identification of players for both fans and journalists and became a common practice in professional baseball.

Since then, numbers on the back of uniforms have become a distinctive and recognizable feature of players on the field.

45

Jon Rauch, a former professional baseball pitcher, is the tallest player in Major League Baseball (MLB) history.

Rauch reached a height of 6 feet 11 inches, which is approximately 210 cm.

His impressive stature earned him the title of the tallest player in MLB history.

Jon Rauch had a career in the Major Leagues that spanned from 2002 to 2013.

He played for several teams during his career, including the Chicago White Sox, Montreal Expos/Washington Nationals, Arizona Diamondbacks, Minnesota Twins, Toronto Blue Jays, New York Mets, and Miami Marlins.

Rauch found success as a pitcher and also had the opportunity to represent the United States in the 2004 Athens Olympics, where he won a gold medal.

On the other hand, batter Eddie Gaedel is known as the shortest player in MLB history.

He measured only 109.2 cm (3 feet 7 inches) tall.

Gaedel made a unique appearance in an MLB baseball game in 1951.

He was hired by the owner of the St. Louis Browns as part of a publicity strategy and became the shortest player to play in an official MLB game.

It is interesting to observe the diversity of sizes and statures found in the world of baseball, which contributes to the richness and variety of the sport.

Both Jon Rauch, the tallest player, and Eddie Gaedel, the shortest player, are prominent examples of the physical diversity found in professional baseball.

46

Alyssa Nakken is a prominent figure in the world of baseball for her historic achievement as the first full-time female coach in Major League Baseball (MLB).

-Beginning of her career: Alyssa Nakken joined the San Francisco Giants organization in January 2014 as an intern in the player development department. Since then, she has proven her worth and advanced in her career in professional baseball.

-Promotion to assistant coach: In January 2020, the Giants announced that Nakken would become an assistant coach for the team. This designation made her the first female coach in the franchise's history and one of the first in the MLB.

-Promotion as a base coach: In July 2020, Alyssa Nakken made history again by being promoted to a base coach for the San Francisco Giants. This marked the first time a woman held a coaching position on the field during an MLB game.

-Role and responsibilities: As a base coach, Nakken works with the Giants players in various aspects, such as skill training and game strategy. She is also involved in the team dynamics, providing support and fostering a positive environment.

-Inspiration and role model: Alyssa Nakken's rise has been a significant milestone in professional baseball and has opened new opportunities for women interested in coaching roles in the Major Leagues. Her presence on the field has inspired many young female baseball players and paved the way for future women in the sport.

47

Jim Abbott was born on September 19, 1967, in Flint, Michigan, United States.

He is known for his career as a baseball pitcher in Major League Baseball (MLB) despite being born without a right hand.

Despite his physical disability, Abbot developed a passion for baseball from an early age.

During his high school education at Flint Central High School, he excelled as a baseball player and caught the attention of scouts from several universities.

Jim Abbott chose to attend the University of Michigan, where he continued playing baseball at the collegiate level.

During his time in college, he set several records and became a standout pitcher.

In 1987, he was part of the United States team that won the gold medal in the Pan American Games.

After his successful college career, Abbott was selected in the first round of the MLB draft in 1988 by the California Angels.

He made his debut in the Major Leagues in 1989 and became the first one-handed pitcher to play in the MLB.

During his career in the Major Leagues, Jim Abbott pitched for the California Angels, New York Yankees, Chicago White Sox, and Milwaukee Brewers.

Throughout his ten seasons in the MLB, Abbott had a record of 87 wins and 108 losses, with an ERA of 4.25.

Additionally, he threw a no-hitter on September 4, 1993, while playing for the Yankees against the Cleveland Indians.

Jim Abbott's determination and talent inspired many people worldwide.

His ability to overcome his disability and succeed in professional baseball made him an example of perseverance and personal triumph.

After retiring from baseball, Abbott has dedicated himself to being a motivational speaker, sharing his story and motivating others to overcome obstacles in their own lives.

Jim Abbott left a significant legacy in baseball and society at large.

His story demonstrates that with determination, hard work, and passion, great things can be achieved, even when facing physical challenges.

48

Cuba has had outstanding success in the World Baseball Cup.

The World Baseball Cup is an international baseball tournament organized by the World Baseball Softball Confederation (WBSC).

It takes place every two years and features the participation of national teams from around the world.

Cuba has been a powerhouse in baseball and has achieved great dominance in the World Baseball Cup over the years.

They have participated in several editions of the tournament and have an impressive record of 25 gold medals out of a total of 31 medals overall.

Cuba's successful streak began in 1939 when they won their first gold medal in the World Baseball Cup held in Havana, Cuba.

Since then, they have continued to enjoy success in the tournament, solidifying their status as one of the top powers in world baseball.

Cuba's consistency in the World Baseball Cup has been remarkable.

They have won gold medals in various editions of the tournament, including those in 1952, 1961, 1969, 1970, 1971, 1972, 1973, 1976, 1984, 1986, 1988, 1990, 1994, 1998, 2001, 2003, and 2005, among others.

In addition to their 25 gold medals, Cuba has also won 3 silver medals and 3 bronze medals in the World Baseball Cup.

Their continued success in the tournament has been a result of the quality of their players, the baseball tradition in the country, and the dedicated focus on the development and training of young talents.

It is important to mention that the World Baseball Cup has evolved over the years and, starting in 2011, has been replaced by the U-23 Baseball World Cup and other international events.

However, Cuba's legacy in the World Baseball Cup remains impressive and reflects their passion and mastery of this sport.

It is worth noting that the United States, despite being one of the most prominent countries in baseball, have obtained fewer medals in the World Baseball Cup compared to Cuba.

They have won a total of 15 medals, of which only four are gold. This further underscores the magnitude of Cuba's achievements in the tournament.

49

At the Tokyo 2020 Olympic Games, Japan achieved a great triumph by winning the gold medal in baseball.

The baseball tournament was part of the Olympic events and took place at various venues in Japan.

In the final of the tournament, Japan faced the United States and won the game with a score of 2-0.

This victory secured Japan's first gold medal in baseball in the history of the Olympic Games.

Previously, Japan had won silver medals in Olympic baseball but had never reached the gold.

On the other hand, the United States, who had won the gold medal at the Sydney 2000 Olympic Games and bronze medals at the Atlanta 1996 and Beijing 2008 Olympic Games, had to settle for the silver medal at the Tokyo 2020 Olympic Games.

Furthermore, in the bronze medal match, the Dominican Republic faced South Korea and managed to defeat them.

Therefore, the Dominican Republic took home the bronze medal in the baseball tournament.

Japan's victory at the Tokyo 2020 Olympic Games was a great achievement for the host country and a significant milestone in the history of Olympic baseball.

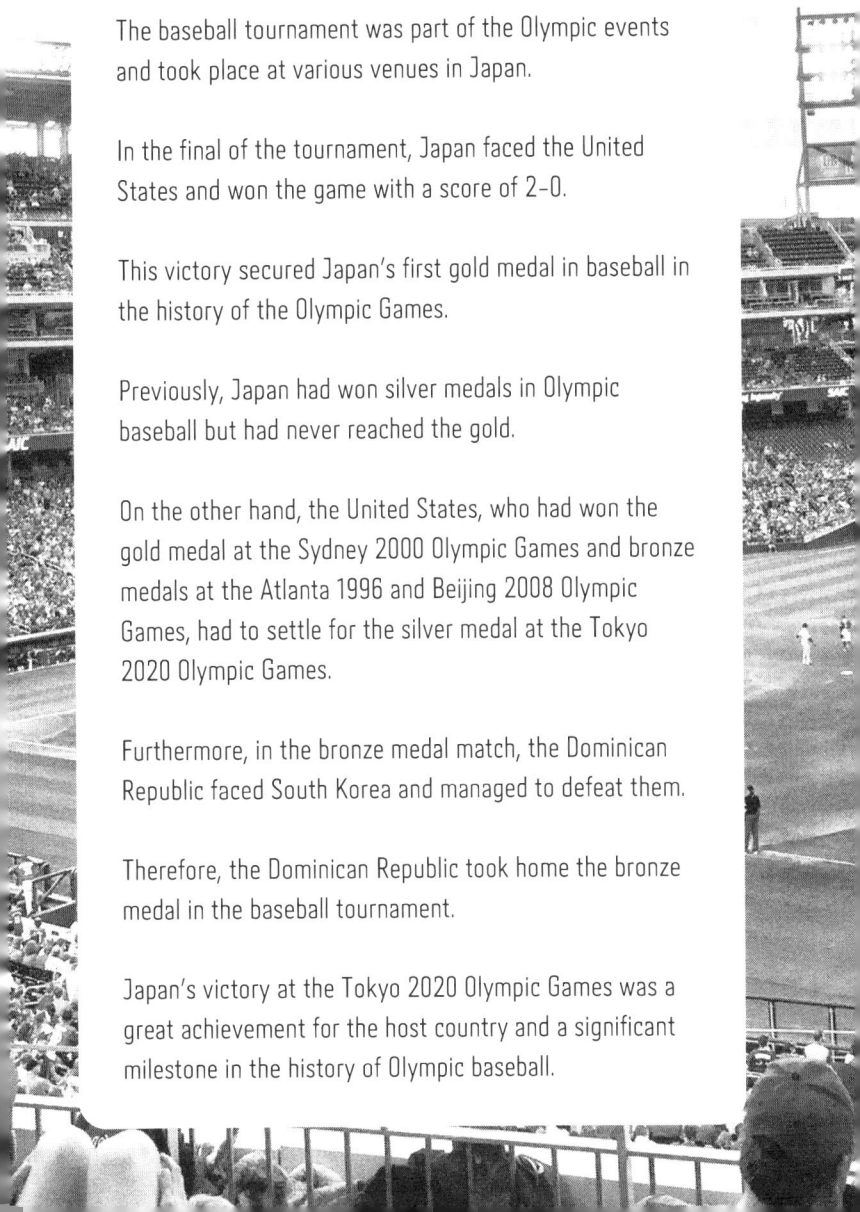

50

Mark McGwire's 70th home run in the 1998 season is one of the most notable moments in baseball history.

This milestone was particularly significant because it set a new record for home runs in a single season, surpassing the previous mark of 61 set by Roger Maris in 1961.

The ball that McGwire hit to achieve that 70th home run became a highly valuable collectible item due to the historical importance of the event.

The ball was retrieved after being caught by a spectator in the stands at Busch Stadium in St. Louis on September 27, 1998.

The ball was subsequently authenticated and certified as McGwire's 70th home run ball.

Since then, it has come to be regarded as an extremely valuable sports artifact.

The current reported price of McGwire's 70th home run ball is approximately $3 million.

However, it is important to note that the prices of collectible items can vary and are subject to market demand and other factors.

The ball itself represents a historic moment in baseball and symbolizes Mark McGwire's career and the 1998 season, which was marked by the competition with Sammy Sosa to break the home run record.

Despite subsequent controversies surrounding the use of steroids in professional baseball, McGwire's 70th home run remains a significant milestone in the sport's history.

51

**Ray Chapman was a professional baseball player who played
for the Cleveland Indians in Major League Baseball (MLB).**

He was born on January 15, 1891, in Kentucky, United States, and played in the MLB from 1912 until his tragic death in 1920.

On August 16, 1920, during a game against the New York Yankees at the Polo Grounds, Ray Chapman was hit in the head by a pitch from Yankees' pitcher Carl Mays.

Chapman couldn't dodge the ball as he was looking towards the pitcher and didn't see Mays' fast and dark delivery coming.

Chapman fell to the ground and was taken to a nearby hospital. Unfortunately, the injuries suffered by Chapman were severe.

Although he initially seemed to be recovering, his condition worsened, and he passed away the next day, on August 17, 1920, at the age of 29.

The official cause of his death was a basal skull fracture due to the impact of the ball.

This tragic incident had a significant impact on baseball and led to changes in the rules and manufacturing of the balls used in MLB.

Prior to Chapman's death, baseballs in the MLB were used for a long time and would become soft, making them difficult to see and harder to hit with power.

This era was known as the "Deadball Era."

After Chapman's death, changes were introduced in the manufacturing of baseballs to make them brighter and easier to see.

Stricter standards were established for the use of new balls during games, and the use of dirty or worn-out balls was prohibited.

These changes helped improve the visibility of the ball and reduce the possibility of similar accidents.

Ray Chapman's death remains the only known case of a professional baseball player dying as a direct result of being hit by a ball during an MLB game.

His tragic incident led to improvements in player safety and a greater emphasis on the visibility and quality of balls used in professional baseball.

52

The duration of a baseball in a game can vary significantly depending on various factors, such as the type of pitches, the speed of the game, and the quality of the ball itself.

In a Major League Baseball (MLB) game, multiple balls are used throughout the match.

This is primarily done to maintain a new and good-condition ball because, during the course of the game, the ball can wear out, get dirty, or get damaged due to pitches, batters, and actions on the field.

Pitchers have the option to request a new ball at any time during their performance if they feel that the current ball is worn out or does not provide them with a proper grip.

Balls that are hit hard and go out of the field or get heavily soiled are also replaced.

It is difficult to determine an exact average number of pitches for the lifespan of a ball in a professional game as it varies widely depending on the aforementioned circumstances.

However, estimates suggest that an average of 70 to 100 balls can be used in a nine-inning MLB game.

This means that a ball can last several pitches before being replaced.

It is important to note that the duration of a baseball can also depend on the quality of its manufacturing and the league's standards.

MLB has strict specifications regarding the characteristics and performance of the balls used in games, and tests are conducted to ensure they meet the required standards.

53

In the 1870s, baseballs were initially made using horsehide.

However, due to the difficulty in obtaining this material, the decision was made to switch to cowhide.

Horsehide was used in the manufacturing of the outer covers of baseballs due to its durability and resilience.

Horse leather was especially resistant to abrasion and could withstand the repeated impact of the game without easily wearing out.

Additionally, the texture and characteristics of horsehide provided a good grip for players when pitching and catching the ball.

However, over time, it became increasingly difficult and costly to obtain enough horsehide to meet the demand for baseballs.

This was due to a combination of factors such as a scarcity of suitable horses for ball production, rising prices, and growing demand for the material for other uses.

As a result, the decision was made to switch to cowhide as an alternative for manufacturing baseballs.

Cowhide is also durable and resilient, although it may have some differences in terms of texture and grip compared to horsehide.

However, baseball manufacturers were able to adapt the manufacturing process and adjust the design of the balls to maintain the desired quality and playing characteristics.

Over the years, various improvements and adjustments have been made to the design and materials used in baseballs.

These changes aim to balance durability, performance, and playing characteristics to ensure an optimal experience for both players and baseball fans.

54

The "Baseball Ball Bounce Test" is used to determine if a ball is ready to be used in a game.

-Testing process: In this test, the baseball is placed in a specially designed air cannon and shot towards a northern white ash wall. The speed at which the ball is launched is 85 feet per second, which is approximately 25.9 meters per second.

-Northern white ash wall material: The northern white ash wall is made of a porous material that allows the ball to bounce more easily and provides a consistent surface for testing. This material helps measure the ball's elasticity and its ability to bounce correctly.

-Bounce requirements: For the ball to pass the test, it must not bounce more than 0.578% of its original velocity. This means that after impacting the northern white ash wall, the ball should not regain more than 0.578% of its initial speed upon bouncing.

-Importance of the test: The bounce test is used to ensure that baseballs have adequate elasticity. If a ball bounces too much or doesn't bounce enough, it can affect the game's performance, the accuracy of pitches, and the safety of the players.

-Baseball ball quality and standards: The bounce test is just one of the many tests and standards applied to baseballs to ensure their quality and uniformity. Other aspects such as weight, size, stitching, compression, and stiffness are also checked to ensure that the balls meet the established standards.

55

The incident where Rick Monday became a national hero took place on April 25, 1976, during a baseball game between the Chicago Cubs and the Los Angeles Dodgers at Dodger Stadium.

During the fourth inning of the game, two men ran onto the field with the intention of burning an American flag.

Rick Monday, who was playing as an outfielder for the Cubs at that time, quickly noticed the situation and headed towards the men.

In an act of bravery, he approached them, snatched the flag from their hands, and protected it from being set on fire.

Rick Monday's heroic gesture was witnessed by the 25,167 fans in the stadium, who rose from their seats and gave him a standing ovation.

As a display of support and patriotism, the spectators started singing the anthem "God Bless America."

The incident was an emotional and symbolic moment that resonated throughout the country, turning Rick Monday into a symbol of love and respect for the American flag.

After the incident, Rick Monday received numerous praises and recognitions for his act of bravery and patriotism.

He was honored with the Congressional Distinguished Citizen Medal by the United States Congress and received numerous awards and accolades throughout his career.

Rick Monday's gesture at Dodger Stadium has become an iconic moment in baseball history and a symbol of respect for national symbols.

His courageous action and defense of the American flag have left a lasting legacy as a national hero and an example of integrity and patriotism in sports.

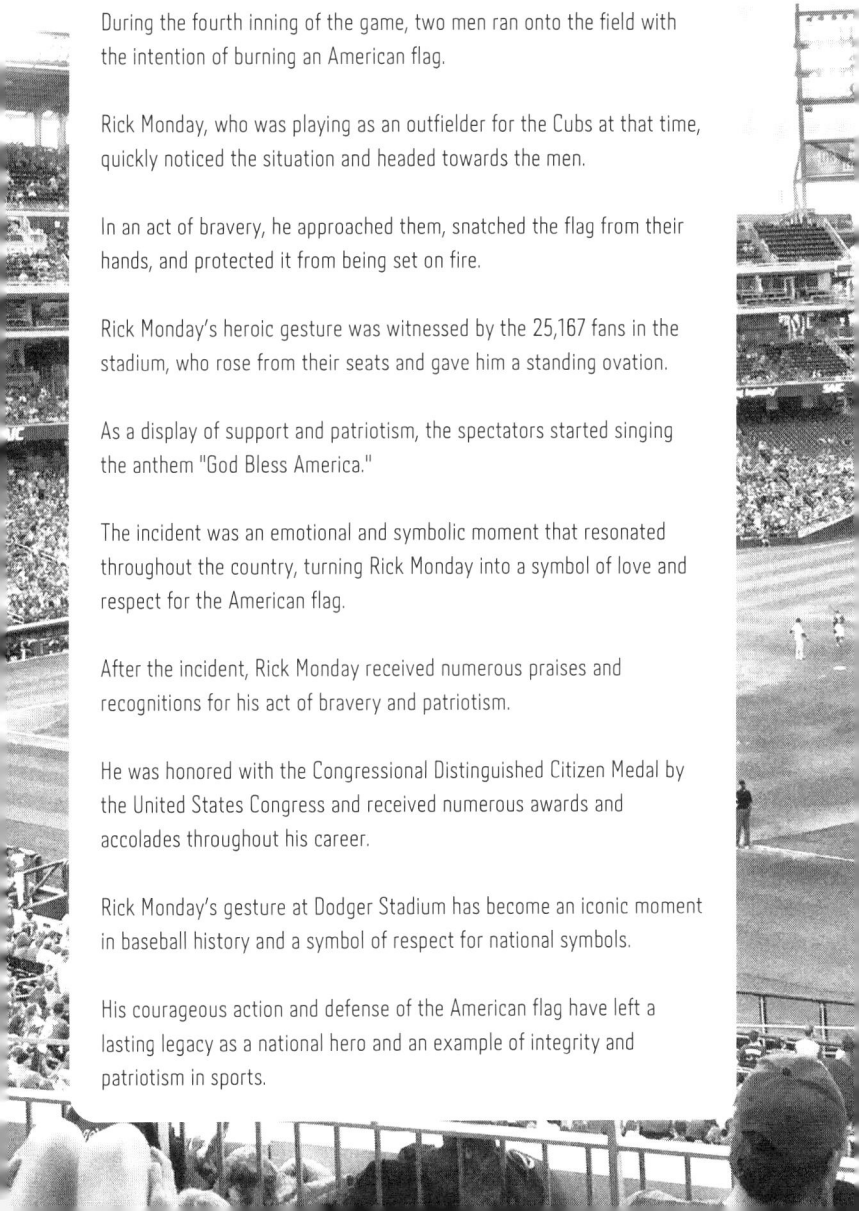

56

The San Francisco Giants team is one of the most prominent teams in Major League Baseball history and has had a notable number of players inducted into the Hall of Fame.

-Orlando Cepeda: Cepeda was an outstanding first baseman and outfielder for the Giants in the 1960s. He was elected to the Hall of Fame in 1999.

-Willie Mays: Considered one of the greatest players of all time, Mays spent the majority of his career with the Giants. He is widely recognized for his defensive skills and offensive power. He was inducted into the Hall of Fame in 1979.

-Juan Marichal: Marichal was one of the most dominant pitchers of his era and spent most of his career in San Francisco. He was elected to the Hall of Fame in 1983.

-Gaylord Perry: Perry, a pitcher, had an outstanding career with multiple teams, including the Giants. He was inducted into the Hall of Fame in 1991.

-Monte Irvin: Irvin was a standout player for the Giants in the 1950s. Although he spent most of his career in the Negro Leagues before integration, he had a significant impact on Major League Baseball. He was elected to the Hall of Fame in 1973.

These are just a few examples of San Francisco Giants players who have been honored with induction into the Hall of Fame.

Other notable players include Carl Hubbell, Mel Ott, and Willie McCovey, among others.

In total, the San Francisco Giants have 24 Hall of Fame members, making them the team with the most players to receive this honor.

This number is a testament to the franchise's legacy and rich history, as well as the talented players who have worn their uniform over the years.

57

Jimmy Piersall. He was a baseball player known for his time with the Boston Red Sox in the 1950s and 1960s.

His Major League career was marked by his talent on the field and his eccentric and sometimes controversial behavior off it.

In August 1963, while playing for the New York Mets, Piersall hit his 100th home run in the Major Leagues.

To celebrate the milestone, Piersall decided to run the bases backward instead of in the usual direction.

This unique way of celebrating the home run became iconic and is remembered as one of the highlights of his career.

In addition to his eccentric behavior, Jimmy Piersall was known for his battle with bipolar disorder, which was then known as manic-depressive illness.

His personal experience with mental illness and his fight against it were documented in the book "Fear Strikes Out," written by Al Hirshberg and published in 1955.

The book was a success and was later adapted into a film of the same name in 1957, starring Anthony Perkins as Piersall.

The book and the film "Fear Strikes Out" narrate the life of Jimmy Piersall, focusing on his relationship with his father and his struggle with bipolar disorder.

Piersall's story helped raise awareness about mental illness and the importance of providing support and understanding to those who experience it.

Jimmy Piersall continued his baseball career after his experience with mental illness, playing for several more teams before retiring in 1967.

Although his career was marked by ups and downs and controversies, his story is still remembered as a testament to personal resilience and a reminder of the importance of mental health in sports and in life in general.

58

Dock Ellis was a professional baseball pitcher who played in the Major Leagues, particularly known for his no-hitter game in 1970 and his admission of pitching under the influence of LSD in that same game.

Dock Ellis was born on March 11, 1945, in Los Angeles, California.

He played for various teams in the Major Leagues but is best remembered for his time with the Pittsburgh Pirates, where he spent the majority of his career.

He was an outstanding pitcher known for his speed and ability to intimidate batters.

On June 12, 1970, Ellis pitched his first and only no-hitter of his career.

That night, he faced the San Diego Padres and accomplished an impressive feat by not allowing any opposing batter to hit a ball throughout the entire game.

However, what makes this achievement even more notable is the later revelation that Ellis was under the influence of LSD during the game.

In subsequent interviews, Ellis admitted that he took LSD on the morning of the game without realizing that he was scheduled to pitch that day.

According to his account, he had difficulty focusing, and his visual and auditory perception were affected by the drug's effects.

Despite the unconventional circumstances, Ellis managed to stay focused enough to pitch a no-hitter.

The story of Ellis' LSD-influenced no-hitter game has captured public attention and has become a famous anecdote in baseball history.

Some have debated whether the drug's effects actually helped or hindered Ellis' performance, but his achievement remains impressive and unique.

After retiring from baseball, Dock Ellis worked in addiction rehabilitation programs and became an advocate for substance abuse prevention.

He passed away on December 19, 2008, due to liver disease.

Despite his ups and downs and controversial choices, Ellis is still remembered as an intriguing character and an important figure in baseball history.

59

On September 28, 1919, the fastest game in the history of Major League Baseball was played.

This encounter took place at the Polo Grounds in New York City and pitted the New York Giants against the Philadelphia Phillies.

The game between the Giants and the Phillies started at 3:00 p.m., and in just 51 minutes, the nine innings were completed.

The Giants emerged victorious with a final score of 6-1 over the Phillies.

The Giants' pitcher, Jesse Barnes, was a key factor in the game's swiftness.

Barnes pitched a complete game, allowing only four hits and one run by the Phillies.

His efficiency on the mound, as well as the good defensive performance by both teams, contributed to the game's quick duration.

In terms of hitting, the Giants were the standout performers.

During the game, they hit efficiently and scored six runs, securing their victory.

In contrast, the Phillies struggled to generate offense and could only score one run during the encounter.

It is important to note that the 51-minute fast game was a rarity at that time and is an exception compared to the average duration of modern baseball games, which typically last around three hours.

Advances in strategy, the pace of the game, and television broadcasts have contributed to an increase in the duration of games in recent decades.

However, the 51-minute game between the New York Giants and the Philadelphia Phillies in 1919 continues to be remembered as a special event and a curiosity in baseball history, demonstrating that, under exceptional circumstances, games can be exceptionally fast and efficient.

60

In 1919, one of the most infamous events in baseball history, known as the 1919 World Series scandal, took place.

The Chicago White Sox, a team from the American League, faced off against the Cincinnati Reds from the National League in that year's World Series.

During the series, eight players from the White Sox were accused of accepting bribes from gamblers to intentionally lose the games.

These players, known as the "Black Sox," included "Shoeless" Joe Jackson, Eddie Cicotte, Oscar "Happy" Felsch, Arnold "Chick" Gandil, Fred McMullin, Charles "Swede" Risberg, George "Buck" Weaver, and Claude "Lefty" Williams.

The scandal came to light after evidence of the illegal betting and corrupt activities of the players was uncovered.

In the aftermath, a trial was held in 1921, where the eight players were acquitted, but the baseball commissioner at the time, Kenesaw Mountain Landis, issued a lifetime ban for the involved players, barring them from participating in any organized baseball activities.

"Shoeless" Joe Jackson, in particular, was one of the most prominent players implicated in the scandal.

He was considered one of the best hitters of his time, and his prowess on the field was noteworthy.

However, despite his talent, Jackson was included in the lifetime ban and never got a chance to play in the Major Leagues again.

In addition to the ban, the events of the 1919 World Series scandal had a significant impact on baseball.

The scandal led to reforms in the sport and resulted in the creation of the position of the baseball commissioner, currently held by Rob Manfred.

It also increased surveillance and security measures to prevent future instances of game-fixing.

Due to Jackson's lifetime ban and the bans on the other players involved in the scandal, none of them have been eligible for induction into the Baseball Hall of Fame.

Although some have argued for Jackson's reinstatement and consideration for the Hall of Fame due to his undeniable talent, to date, no changes have been made to his status.

61

Researchers have conducted studies on the ability of successful baseball batters to rapidly and accurately process visual information.

These studies have revealed that these batters possess certain perceptual and cognitive skills that enable them to track the ball better and make faster decisions at the plate.

One key aspect of successful batters' ability is their capacity to detect the spin of the ball as soon as the pitcher releases it.

The spin of the ball is important because it affects its trajectory and movement in the air.

By being able to detect the spin, batters can better anticipate the location and type of pitch they are facing.

Successful batters have been found to perceive the ball in "slightly slower motion" compared to average players.

This means they have sharper visual perception and can process visual information more quickly.

They can pick up subtle details of the ball's trajectory, such as speed, direction, and movement, giving them an advantage when deciding whether to swing at the ball or not.

The ability to process visual information quickly and accurately is related to experience and practice.

Successful batters have spent countless hours at the plate, facing different pitchers and types of pitches.

Over the years, they have developed an ability to recognize patterns and anticipate movements based on the visual cues they receive.

Additionally, the ability to process visual information is also related to neurological and genetic factors.

Some studies suggest that certain brain traits, such as visual processing speed and selective attention capacity, can influence a batter's ability to effectively detect and react to the ball.

62

Eddie Gaedel. Born on June 8, 1925, and died on June 18, 1961, he is known as the shortest player to ever participate in a Major League Baseball game.

He measured 3 feet 7 inches in height.

His appearance in the game took place on August 19, 1951, as part of a publicity stunt organized by Bill Veeck, the owner of the St. Louis Browns team.

In that game, the St. Louis Browns were playing against the Detroit Tigers at Sportsman's Park in St. Louis.

Bill Veeck intended to increase attendance at the game and generate publicity by introducing Eddie Gaedel as a batter.

Gaedel wore the jersey number "1/8" on his uniform.

When his turn came to bat in the bottom of the first inning, Gaedel took his position at the plate.

He had a specially-made bat for him and a strike zone adjusted to make it difficult for the pitcher to throw accurately to him.

The Detroit Tigers' pitcher, Bob Cain, had difficulty throwing strikes to Gaedel due to his small stature and the modified strike zone.

Eventually, Cain threw four consecutive pitches that were balls, and Gaedel walked to first base.

After his appearance at the plate, he was replaced by a pinch runner and never played in the Major Leagues again.

Eddie Gaedel's appearance in the game generated a lot of media attention and became a historic moment in baseball.

Although it was a one-time event and a publicity stunt, his participation is still remembered to this day.

63

Julio Franco.

Born on August 23, 1958, he is known for being the oldest player to hit a home run in Major League Baseball.

Franco played for several teams throughout his career, including the New York Mets.

On April 20, 2006, while playing for the New York Mets, Franco hit a home run at the age of 47 years and 240 days.

It was a remarkable achievement, as most players retire long before reaching that age.

The home run came against San Diego Padres pitcher Chan Ho Park. Franco was known for his longevity in baseball and his dedication to physical fitness.

He played in the Major Leagues for a span of 23 years, from 1982 to 2007.

Throughout his career, he also played for other notable teams such as the Cleveland Indians, Texas Rangers, and Atlanta Braves.

In addition to his ability to hit home runs at an advanced age, Franco was known for his unique batting style and his ability to make contact with the ball.

He was also a versatile player who played multiple positions throughout his career, including first base, second base, and designated hitter.

Julio Franco became an example of longevity in baseball and demonstrated that age is not always a barrier to success in the sport.

His record of being the oldest player to hit a home run remains an impressive milestone in baseball history.

64

Throwing a baseball at speeds exceeding 100 mph is certainly challenging and rarely achieved by most pitchers, however, it is not completely impossible.

Throughout the history of baseball, there have been pitchers who have managed to reach and surpass this mark.

It is important to note that throwing at extremely high speeds puts a significant strain on a pitcher's arm and shoulder.

The biomechanics of throwing a baseball at high velocity is a complex and highly demanding process in terms of strength and coordination.

To achieve speeds exceeding 100 mph, pitchers must have a combination of factors, including efficient pitching mechanics, proper technique, good strength and conditioning, as well as favorable genetics.

These pitchers often possess a unique combination of strength, flexibility, and coordination that enables them to generate exceptional velocity.

However, it is also true that throwing at extreme speeds can increase the risk of arm injuries for the pitcher.

The force generated by the pitching motion can exert significant stress on the tendons, ligaments, and muscles of the arm.

Excessive repeated torsion and overload can lead to injuries such as tendon tears, ligament issues, and shoulder and elbow problems.

To minimize the risk of injuries, professional and amateur pitchers receive training in safe and efficient pitching techniques, and they also follow specific conditioning programs to strengthen the muscles of the arm and shoulder, as well as to maintain good flexibility and prevent muscle imbalances.

65

**The curveball is a baseball pitch that has a characteristic
curve movement towards the plate.**

When thrown correctly, the curveball can deviate significantly from a straight line and confuse batters.

The amount of curve in a curveball can vary depending on the pitcher and their ability to throw it.

Generally, a good curveball is considered to curve between 12 and 20 inches from a straight line towards the plate.

Therefore, it is certainly possible for a curveball to curve more than 17 inches.

The curving effect in a curveball is achieved through the pitcher's grip and throwing technique.

The pitcher grips the ball in a way that the fingers apply pressure on it, creating a forward spin.

As the ball leaves the pitcher's hand, the spinning effect and arm motion generate the curve.

The trajectory and velocity of a curveball can vary depending on the pitcher.

Some pitchers may throw the curveball with a faster pace, making it harder to detect by the batter.

Others may emphasize more on the drop or the lateral sweep in the curve.

Batters must read and anticipate the curveball in order to effectively make contact with it.

A well-thrown curveball can deceive the batter and make them hit the ball late, resulting in missed contact or producing a weak hit.

It is important to note that throwing an effective curveball requires practice, skill, and control from the pitcher.

There can also be variations in the curve depending on the speed, release angle, and individual technique of the pitcher.

66

Harry Wright.

He was a former cricket player and businessman who played a crucial role in the early history of baseball.

He was born on January 10, 1835, in Sheffield, England, and passed away on October 3, 1895, in Atlantic City, New Jersey.

Wright is primarily known for organizing and managing the first professional baseball team, the Cincinnati Red Stockings, in 1869.

Prior to this, baseball was mostly an amateur sport, but Wright sought to create a professional team that could compete at a more serious and sustainable level.

Wright, along with his younger brother George Wright, who was also a talented baseball player, gathered a group of skilled players and signed them to paid contracts.

The Red Stockings thus became the first fully professional team in the history of baseball.

In 1869, Harry Wright signed contracts with nine players for the Red Stockings, with an average annual salary of $950, a significant figure at that time.

This approach of hiring players and paying them a salary established the model for modern professional baseball.

On March 15, 1869, the Cincinnati Red Stockings played their first official game against the Antioch College team.

In that game, the Red Stockings showcased their dominance by winning with an overwhelming score of 41-7.

This initial success helped popularize the team and the concept of professional baseball overall.

The Red Stockings continued their dominance in the following years, achieving an undefeated streak of 81 consecutive victories in 1869 and 1870.

However, financial pressure and competition from other professional teams led to the dissolution of the team after the 1870 season.

After his time with the Red Stockings, Harry Wright continued his baseball career as a player and manager for various teams.

In 1876, he became the player-manager of the Boston Red Stockings (now known as the Atlanta Braves), a team in the newly formed National League.

Under his leadership, the Red Stockings won four consecutive National League titles from 1877 to 1880.

67

The Deadball Era, also known as the Deadball period, refers to a specific period in baseball history that roughly spanned from 1900 to 1919.

During this time, the baseballs used in games were notoriously soft and loose compared to modern baseballs.

This had a significant impact on how baseball was played and the balance between pitchers and batters.

The main characteristic of the deadball was its lack of elasticity and hardness, making it difficult for batters to hit the ball far.

These balls were heavier and lacked the bounce that more modern balls possess.

As a result, pitchers of the era had a clear advantage over batters as they could manipulate and control the ball more effectively.

Several standout pitchers emerged during the Deadball Era, including names like Cy Young, Walter Johnson, and Grover Cleveland.

These pitchers were known for their control, speed, and mastery on the mound.

Taking advantage of the difficulty of hitting deadballs, these pitchers achieved impressive statistics and records that still stand today.

Despite the advantage of pitchers, there were also prolific hitters during this period.

Legendary players like Ty Cobb, Joe Jackson, and Honus Wagner managed to excel despite the challenges of hitting the deadball.

These talented batters showcased exceptional skills and became icons of baseball in their era.

In addition to the ball characteristics, other factors contributed to the Deadball Era.

Baseball stadiums of the time were generally larger and more spacious, further hindering home runs and favoring a style of play based on base running, contact hitting, and defensive strategies.

The Deadball Era gradually came to an end starting in the 1920s when baseballs began to be manufactured with more solid materials and features that allowed for more powerful hitting.

This, along with changes in rules and the evolution of gameplay strategies, contributed to the era of modern baseball with a greater emphasis on power hitting.

68

**A labrum tear is a serious shoulder injury
that can affect baseball pitchers.**

The labrum is a ring of cartilage that surrounds the shoulder socket and
helps stabilize the joint.

When a labrum tear occurs, the cartilage separates from its normal
position, which can cause pain, weakness, and limited range of motion.

For a baseball pitcher, a labrum tear can be particularly problematic as
the repetitive force and stress on the shoulder during pitching can
aggravate the injury and hinder recovery.

This injury is considered one of the worst for pitchers due to its negative
effects on performance and career prospects.

A torn labrum generally requires surgery to repair or reconstruct the
damaged cartilage.

Labrum repair surgery involves reattaching the torn cartilage to its
original position, while labrum reconstruction involves replacing the
damaged tissue with tissue from other areas of the body or with grafts.

Rehabilitation after surgery can be a long and challenging process as
time is required for the shoulder to heal and fully recover.

It is important to note that each case of a labrum tear is unique, and
recovery may vary from player to player.

Some pitchers may return to the game after surgery and have a
successful career, while others may struggle with the injury and
experience difficulties in their performance.

The ability to recover and succeed after a labrum tear may also
depend on factors such as the severity of the injury, compliance
with rehabilitation and strengthening work, as well as the
player's age and overall physical condition.

69

The catcher is one of the key players on the field.

Their primary position is to receive pitches from the pitcher and catch the ball.

However, this task is not easy and requires special skills and physical endurance.

Challenges faced by catchers in baseball:

–Circulatory issues in the hand: When catching powerful pitches, catchers have to absorb the force of the ball with their glove. Although gloves are designed with additional padding to protect the hands, catchers are still exposed to a significant amount of repetitive impact. This constant pressure and impacts can cause circulatory issues in the hand, such as reduced blood flow and sensitivity.

–Meniscus injuries: The meniscus is a cartilage in the knee that helps cushion and stabilize the joint. Due to the physical demands of the catcher position, players are often squatting or crouching for long periods of time. This can exert significant pressure on the knees and increase the risk of meniscus injuries. A torn meniscus can be extremely painful and limit the catcher's ability to make quick and agile movements behind the plate.

In addition to these mentioned, catchers also face other common risks in baseball, such as being hit by a bat or a stray ball, collisions with runners attempting to score, and overall wear and tear on the body due to the physical rigor of the game.

Despite these challenges, catchers are a vital part of any baseball team.

Their ability to call plays, work closely with pitchers, and defend the strike zone is crucial to the team's success.

Many catchers are admired for their physical and mental endurance, as well as their ability to stay calm and lead the team from behind the plate.

70

The expression "tools of ignorance" is a colloquial phrase used in baseball to describe a catcher's equipment.

However, it's important to note that this phrase is a kind of joke or play on words and doesn't actually reflect the reality or intellectual abilities of catchers.

The job of a baseball catcher is considered one of the most difficult and demanding in the sport.

It requires a combination of physical and mental skills to properly perform their tasks.

Some of the skills needed to be a good catcher include:

-Defensive skills: Catchers must have good ability to catch pitches, including those that are fast, curving, or difficult to handle. They must also be adept at blocking pitches in the dirt to prevent runners from advancing and throwing with accuracy to try to catch stealing runners.

-Game knowledge: Catchers must have a deep understanding of the game and a good ability to read situations on the field. They should be able to communicate with pitchers and the rest of the team, make quick and strategic decisions, and be able to adapt to different pitching styles and game situations.

-Physical and mental endurance: The work of a catcher can be physically exhausting as they have to squat for long periods of time, endure the impact of thrown balls, and suffer general wear and tear on the body. They must also have the ability to maintain focus and calm under pressure, as a small lapse of attention or mistake can have significant consequences in the game.

71

Glen Gorbous was a professional baseball player known for his record in the longest throw in the history of the sport.

-Record throw: During an exhibition throw in 1957, Glen Gorbous set the record for the longest throw made by a professional baseball player. With a running start, he threw the ball an impressive distance of 445 feet, 10 inches (136 meters).

-Historical context: Gorbous' record throw took place at a time when distance measurements were not as precise as they are today. Although there wasn't modern technology to accurately measure the distance of a throw, his mark remains impressive and is considered one of the longest throws in baseball history.

-Professional career: Glen Gorbous played in Major League Baseball (MLB) as an outfielder and pitcher for the Detroit Tigers and Milwaukee Braves. While he didn't have a highly distinguished career in terms of statistics, his record throw earned him a place in the annals of baseball and he is remembered for his singular feat.

-Importance of the throw: Gorbous' record throw highlights both the physical strength and athletic ability required to throw the ball long distances. Throwing in baseball is one of the fundamental skills, and its mastery is crucial for both pitchers and players in other positions.

72

In the 1880s, baseball was undergoing significant changes in terms of uniforms and players' appearance.

- **Position-based colored jerseys:** In 1882, players used to wear distinctive colored jerseys based on the position they played instead of wearing the team's uniform. This helped quickly identify a player's position on the field. For example, pitchers could wear a certain color jersey while outfielders could wear another.

- **Introduction of team uniforms:** In 1883, team owners ruled that each team had the freedom to choose their own uniform, allowing for greater customization and promotion of team identity. However, there was one exception: the stockings, or socks, were still determined by the leagues. This was done to maintain some uniformity in players' appearance and avoid confusion on the field.

This change allowed teams to have their own visual identity and provided them the opportunity to design uniforms that reflected the colors and spirit of their city or team.

As the 20th century progressed, baseball uniforms became an essential part of team and player identity.

Uniforms included jerseys with the player's name and number, caps, pants, and socks, all designed to represent the organization and unify the team's appearance.

73

"Cranks" were a term used to refer to baseball fans in the late 1880s in the United States.

It is said that the term "fan" is a shortened form of "crank," which originally had a different meaning.

The term "crank" was previously used to describe an eccentric person or someone obsessed with a particular topic.

In the context of baseball, "Cranks" were passionate and enthusiastic fans of the game who often showed extreme devotion to their favorite teams.

During that time, baseball was growing in popularity and becoming a highly followed sport.

The "Cranks" stood out for their enthusiasm and devotion to the game.

They were known for attending games, cheering loudly and passionately, and closely following baseball statistics and news.

The term "crank" began to fall out of use as baseball established itself as a more popular sport, and the use of the word "fan" became popular to refer to fans.

Although the terms "crank" and "fan" were initially used interchangeably, over time "fan" became the more commonly used term to describe baseball and other sports followers.

Today, the term "fan" is widely used to describe passionate followers of any sport, team, or activity in general.

The word "fan" has become part of common vocabulary and is used worldwide to refer to enthusiastic fans.

74

Henry Chadwick, known as the "father of baseball," was a prominent 19th-century sports journalist whose work and contributions helped popularize and shape baseball as we know it today.

-Journalism career: Henry Chadwick was born on October 5, 1824, in England and moved to the United States in his youth. He began his journalism career as a writer and editor for the New York Clipper, a sports newspaper of the time. Chadwick specialized in baseball coverage and became an influential figure in the field of sports journalism.

-Popularizing baseball: Through his articles and reporting, Chadwick greatly contributed to the popularization of baseball in the United States. His writings were accessible and appealing to readers, helping spread enthusiasm for the sport across the country. Chadwick believed that baseball was a game that fostered positive values such as sportsmanship and teamwork.

-Invention of the box score: One of Chadwick's most significant contributions to baseball was the invention of an early version of the box score, a way to record and present game statistics. Before his invention, baseball game records were rudimentary and lacked the organization and detail we know today. Chadwick developed a system to orderly record and present key actions in a game, such as batters, pitchers, outs, and runs scored.

-Role in rule codification: Chadwick also played a crucial role in codifying baseball rules. He was one of the main advocates for developing a set of uniform rules for the game, allowing for greater standardization and understanding of the sport nationwide. His work helped lay the foundation for modern baseball and establish a regulatory framework still used today.

-Induction into the Baseball Hall of Fame: Henry Chadwick is the only sports journalist to have been elected to the Baseball Hall of Fame in Cooperstown, New York. He was included in the inaugural class of 1938 as recognition for his influence and contributions to the development and spread of baseball.

75

Cal Ripken Jr.

Known as the "Iron Man" for his incredible durability and consecutive games played record in Major League Baseball, Cal Ripken Jr. is one of the most prominent players in the sport's history.

Calvin Edwin Ripken Jr. was born on August 24, 1960, in Havre de Grace, Maryland, United States.

He is the son of former baseball player Cal Ripken Sr. and the brother of fellow baseball player Billy Ripken. Cal Ripken Jr. is considered one of the greatest shortstops in baseball history.

–Consecutive games played record: Cal Ripken Jr.'s most notable achievement is his record of 2,632 consecutive games played. This record surpassed the previous record of 2,130 consecutive games set by Lou Gehrig in 1939. Ripken achieved this incredible feat by not missing a single game from May 30, 1982, to September 19, 1998, spanning 16 complete seasons.

–American League Most Valuable Player: Cal Ripken Jr. was named the Most Valuable Player (MVP) of the American League on two occasions. The first time was in 1983 when he had an outstanding season both defensively and offensively, leading the Baltimore Orioles to win the World Series. The second time was in 1991 when Ripken had a standout performance at shortstop and was a productive hitter.

–Other accomplishments and recognitions: In addition to his consecutive games played record and MVP awards, Cal Ripken Jr. accumulated many other accomplishments and recognitions throughout his career. He was selected to the All-Star Game 19 times and won two Gold Gloves as the best defensive shortstop in the American League. He was also inducted into the Baseball Hall of Fame in 2007 in his first year of eligibility.

–Legacy and contributions: Cal Ripken Jr. left a lasting legacy in baseball, both for his on-field ability and his work ethic and dedication to the game. His consecutive games played record is considered one of the most impressive achievements in sports history and has become a symbol of durability and commitment for baseball players worldwide.

76

Pete Rose, born on April 14, 1941, in Cincinnati, Ohio,
is a controversial figure in baseball history.

-Career and records: He is renowned for his outstanding career in
Major League Baseball, primarily with the Cincinnati Reds. He played
in the majors from 1963 to 1986 and then had a brief comeback in
1987 as a player and player-manager with the Reds. During his career,
Rose set two historic records: most hits (4,256) and most games
played (3,562). His ability to make contact with the ball and his
durability on the field earned him recognition and admiration.

-Gambling and ban: In 1989, Pete Rose faced a series of accusations
related to gambling on baseball games while he was the manager of
the Cincinnati Reds. The investigation concluded that he had bet on
several games involving his own team. In August 1989, Rose reached
an agreement with the Office of the Commissioner of Baseball in
which he admitted the accusations and accepted a lifetime ban from
baseball. This made him the only player to be permanently banned
from the sport.

-Controversy and debate: Pete Rose's ban sparked heated debate in
the baseball world. While many recognize his accomplishments as a
player and his hits record, his involvement in gambling is considered
to have violated one of the fundamental rules of the sport and
undermined the integrity of the game. Over the years, there have been
discussions and petitions for Rose to be reinstated and eligible for the
Baseball Hall of Fame, but so far, no changes have been made to his
status.

-Life after baseball: After his ban from baseball, Pete Rose has been
involved in various business ventures and activities related to the
sport. He has worked as a sports commentator, participated in public
appearances, and been involved in promotional activities. However,
his eligibility for the Baseball Hall of Fame remains a controversial
topic, and he has not been included in regular voting.

77

Richie Ashburn was an outstanding American baseball player who played in the Major Leagues during the 1940s and 1950s.

He is remembered for his career with the Philadelphia Phillies, where he played as a center fielder and became one of the most beloved and respected players in the franchise's history.

Regarding the specific incident you mentioned, it occurred on August 17, 1957, during a game between the Philadelphia Phillies and the New York Giants at the Polo Grounds.

During that game, Ashburn was at bat and hit two consecutive foul balls that ended up hitting a woman named Alice Roth in the stands.

The first foul ball hit Alice Roth in the nose, fracturing it.

As doctors attended to her and carried her on a stretcher out of the stadium, Ashburn hit another foul ball that unexpectedly struck Roth again, this time hitting her in the leg.

This incident has become famous and is considered a notable event in baseball history.

Although it was an unfortunate and accidental situation, it captured media attention and has been told as a curious anecdote in Richie Ashburn's career.

Ashburn was known for being a skilled and disciplined player.

He was an outstanding hitter, with a career batting average of .308.

He was also known for his defensive ability in center field, winning the Gold Glove Award three times.

After retiring as a player, Ashburn became a radio and television commentator for the Philadelphia Phillies and was highly respected for his knowledge of the game and friendly style.

He was inducted into the Baseball Hall of Fame in 1995, in recognition of his outstanding career as a player.

78

In 1943, during World War II, Major League Baseball in the United States was affected by a shortage of male players due to military service.

In that context, Philip Wrigley, owner of the Chicago Cubs, decided to create a professional women's softball team with the aim of keeping fans' interest in baseball alive and, at the same time, providing an opportunity for women to play sports professionally.

This team was originally known as the "Chicago Girls' Softball Cubs" and became one of the founding teams of the All-American Girls Softball League (AAGSL).

The team played at Wrigley Field, the Cubs' stadium, and was expected to attract fans who still longed for baseball during the war.

In its early seasons, the game was played under softball rules, which involved underhand pitching.

However, as time went on and the players' talent increased, it was decided that the game would switch to baseball, using the traditional overhand pitching rules.

With the switch to baseball, the team's name was also modified to become the All-American Girls Baseball League (AAGBL) in 1949.

The league expanded and eventually had teams in various cities across the United States and Canada, such as the Rockford Peaches, Racine Belles, Kenosha Comets, and South Bend Blue Sox, among others.

The league's success grew over the years, and the players, known as the "baseball girls," began to attract a considerable audience.

Although initially a temporary strategy to fill the void left by male players, the AAGBL proved to be popular and successful.

However, after the 1954 season, the AAGBL disbanded due to declining attendance and financial difficulties.

Although the league came to an end, it left a significant legacy by demonstrating that women could also play baseball at a professional level and entertain fans.

The story of the All-American Girls Baseball League gained national and international recognition with the 1992 film "A League of Their Own," starring Tom Hanks, Geena Davis, and Madonna.

The film tells the story of the league and highlights the challenges and achievements of the women who participated in it.

79

The diamond pattern on a baseball field is a distinctive design created by mowing the grass in different directions.

This technique is used to give the playing field an attractive and unique visual appearance.

To achieve this pattern, special lawn mowers equipped with rollers are used.

These rollers have blades that cut the grass at different heights and slightly push the grass in different directions.

When the roller pushes the grass forward, it is similar to vacuuming a plush carpet.

This forward movement of the grass creates a visual effect where the grass blades bend away from the viewer.

These bent blades capture more light and appear lighter in comparison to the blades that bend toward the viewer.

On the other hand, when the roller pushes the grass in the opposite direction, the grass blades bend toward the viewer.

These bent blades facing the viewer appear darker because the light reflects differently on them.

The final result of this mowing process in different directions is a diamond pattern on the baseball field's grass.

This technique is used to enhance the field's appearance and add an aesthetically pleasing look during games.

It is important to note that the diamond pattern technique does not affect the performance of the game or have a significant impact on how baseball is played.

Its main purpose is to provide a visually pleasing appearance for spectators and highlight the field's aesthetics.

80

Jackie Robinson is widely recognized as the first African American baseball player in Major League Baseball in the modern era.

On April 15, 1947, Robinson broke the color barrier by making his debut with the Brooklyn Dodgers, marking a significant milestone in the history of sports and civil rights.

However, there are historical records indicating that there was another African American player who played in the Major Leagues before Robinson.

This player was named William Edward White, and his only game in the Major Leagues was on June 21, 1879, when he played as a first baseman for the Providence Grays of the National League.

It is important to note that the context and circumstances in which White played differ significantly from Jackie Robinson's experience.

At that time, racial segregation was prevalent in American society and professional baseball.

White, however, did not have to face the same difficulties and systematic discrimination that Robinson and other African American players faced in the 20th century.

Additionally, historical records about White's game are limited, and information about his race was not widely known or recognized at that time.

Therefore, although White technically played in the Major Leagues before Robinson, his historical contribution to the desegregation of baseball was not acknowledged at the time nor has it been widely publicized.

81

The record for the fastest baseball pitch by a woman is 69 mph (111.05 km/h).

This mark was achieved by Lauren Boden, a softball player from the United States, on September 20, 2013.

Lauren Boden set this record on the set of the TV show "Officially Amazing" in Claremont, California, USA.

During the show, Boden showcased her skill and power by throwing the ball at an impressive speed, surpassing other competitors and setting a new world record.

It is important to note that this record specifically refers to the pitch speed of a woman in the sport of baseball or softball.

In general, pitch speeds in baseball vary depending on the gender, category, and level of play.

In men's professional baseball, for example, pitchers often reach speeds higher than those of female baseball or softball players.

82

The history of Major League Baseball (MLB) dates back to the late 19th century.

During its early seasons, the league featured several original teams that laid the groundwork for the development and expansion of professional baseball in the United States.

These are the eight original MLB teams:

–Philadelphia Athletics: Founded in 1860, the Philadelphia Athletics were one of the original teams in the league. Although the team originally belonged to the Philadelphia Athletics Association, they joined the National League in 1876 and became founding members of the MLB.

–St. Louis Brown Stockings: Founded in 1875, the St. Louis Brown Stockings were one of the original teams in the National League. Later, the team changed its name to the St. Louis Browns and eventually relocated to Baltimore in 1954 to become the Baltimore Orioles.

–Hartford Dark Blues: Founded in 1874, the Hartford Dark Blues were one of the original teams in the National League. However, the team had a brief existence and dissolved after the 1877 season.

–Louisville Grays: Founded in 1876, the Louisville Grays were also one of the original teams in the National League. However, the team faced financial difficulties and withdrew from the league after the 1877 season.

–Mutual of New York: Founded in 1871, the New York Mutuals were one of the original teams in the precursor league to the National League. However, the team dissolved after the 1876 season.

–Boston Red Stockings: Founded in 1871, the Boston Red Stockings were one of the original teams in the precursor league to the National League. The team had early success and became one of the prominent teams in the early years of professional baseball. Later, the team changed its name to the Boston Braves and eventually relocated to Atlanta in 1966 to become the Atlanta Braves.

–Cincinnati Red Stockings: Founded in 1881, the Cincinnati Red Stockings were one of the original teams in the National League. Although the team changed its name multiple times over the years, it is considered one of the predecessors to the current Cincinnati Reds.

–Chicago White Stockings: Founded in 1870, the Chicago White Stockings were one of the original teams in the precursor league to the National League. Later, the team changed its name to the Chicago Cubs and became one of the most iconic and beloved teams in baseball history.

83

The Baseball Hall of Fame is an institution that honors players, coaches, executives, and notable personalities in baseball who have had a significant impact on the sport.

There are two main ways to select members for the Hall of Fame:

-Election by the Baseball Writers' Association of America (BBWAA):
The BBWAA is an organization composed of journalists and writers specializing in baseball. Each year, BBWAA members receive ballots to vote for eligible candidates for the Hall of Fame. To be eligible for BBWAA voting, a player must have been retired from professional baseball for at least five years.
BBWAA members must have at least ten years of experience in baseball coverage to be eligible to vote. Each member can vote for up to ten players on their ballot. To be elected, a player must receive at least 75% of the votes from BBWAA members participating in the election. However, there is an exclusion clause in the BBWAA voting. If an eligible player does not receive at least 5% of the votes in a given election, they are automatically eliminated from any future consideration on BBWAA ballots.

-Veterans Committee: In addition to the BBWAA voting, there are several veterans committees that review and consider candidates who were not elected by the BBWAA in their timely manner. These committees include the Early Baseball Era Committee (1871-1949), the Golden Era Committee (1950-1969), and the Modern Baseball Era Committee (1970-1987). Each committee meets at regular intervals to evaluate candidates and vote for their inclusion in the Hall of Fame.

It is important to note that the election to the Hall of Fame is a rigorous process, and voters consider a variety of factors, such as individual statistics, on-field achievements, impact on the game, and the player's integrity.

Each year, the voting results are announced, and the newly elected members are honored in a special ceremony in Cooperstown, New York, where the Baseball Hall of Fame is located.

84

Baseball players in the minor leagues generally receive significantly lower salaries compared to Major League players.

The salary structure in the minor leagues is quite different and varies based on the level of play and the team organization.

-**Off-season and Spring Training Salary:** During the off-season and spring training, minor league players do not receive a salary. However, the team organization typically provides them with housing and a daily allowance to cover their basic needs. In some cases, this daily allowance can be around $10.

-**Regular Season Salary:** During the regular season, minor league players receive a monthly salary. However, these salaries are significantly lower than those of Major League players. The salary amounts in the minor leagues vary depending on the level they play at. Minor league levels include Class A, Advanced Class A, Double-A, and Triple-A, among others. In general, salaries in the minor leagues are modest and can range from $1,160 to $2,100 per month. These amounts may vary and are subject to change. Additionally, some players may receive additional bonuses, such as signing bonuses or performance incentives.

It is important to note that these salaries may not be sufficient to cover all the financial needs of minor league players.

Many minor league players face economic challenges and rely on other means, such as working secondary jobs or receiving financial support from their families, to supplement their income.

It is worth noting that in recent years, there has been a greater focus on improving the conditions and salaries of minor league players.

Major League Baseball (MLB) and the MLB Players Association have been working on initiatives to increase salaries and improve living conditions for players in the minor leagues.

These efforts are aimed at providing greater financial support and improving the quality of life for players aspiring to reach the Major Leagues.

85

In the history of baseball, there have been notable and unusual trades.

–Johnny Jones for a 25-pound turkey: In 1931, the Chattanooga Shortstop, a minor league team, traded player Johnny Jones to the Charlotte Hornets in exchange for a 25-pound turkey. This trade is remembered as one of the most unusual in baseball history due to the unconventional nature of the "asset" involved.

–Jack Fenton for a bag of prunes: Another unusual trade occurred when Jack Fenton, a player in the Pacific Coast League, was transferred to the San Francisco team in exchange for a bag of prunes. This trade is famous for its extravagance and has become a peculiar anecdote in baseball history.

–Babe Ruth for $125,000: The most famous and significant trade in baseball history took place in 1919 when the New York Yankees acquired the legendary Babe Ruth from the Boston Red Sox in exchange for $125,000. This trade has become a historic milestone because it marked the beginning of the "Curse of the Bambino," as the Red Sox went several decades without winning a World Series after parting ways with Ruth, while the Yankees became a baseball powerhouse.

It is important to note that these trades are notable examples of unusual situations in baseball but do not represent the norm in most trades.

Most trades in professional baseball involve players, cash, future draft picks, or other assets that have a more conventional sporting value.

86

Benny Distefano is known for being the last left-handed catcher to play in Major League Baseball.

In 1989, he had the opportunity to serve as a catcher in three games for the Pittsburgh Pirates.

His brief appearance as a catcher made history, as left-handed players in that position are quite unusual in baseball.

As for left-handed pitchers caught by left-handed catchers in at least one defensive inning, it is estimated that there have been around 30 cases in the history of Major League Baseball.

This means that only a handful of left-handed pitchers have had the experience of being caught by a left-handed catcher in a Major League game.

If we expand the criteria to left-handed catchers who have caught at least 100 games throughout their career, the number decreases even further.

According to records, there have been only around 5 left-handed catchers who have reached that milestone in the history of Major League Baseball.

These players have been a rarity in the catcher position and have made their mark on the game.

87

The real name of Yogi Berra, the famous professional baseball catcher, is Lawrence Peter Berra.

The nickname "Yogi" was given to Berra during his teenage years and has been his recognized name ever since.

The story behind Yogi Berra's nickname goes back to his time playing baseball in the American Legion.

After attending a movie with his friend Jack Maguire, the latter noticed a resemblance between Berra and a "yogi," a term used to describe a person who practices yoga and seeks spiritual enlightenment.

Maguire jokingly said, "I'm going to call you Yogi."

From that moment on, the nickname stuck and became the most recognized way to refer to Lawrence Peter Berra.

Yogi Berra's nickname became so popular that it ended up being the name he was known by in the world of baseball and beyond.

Yogi Berra is widely recognized as one of the most prominent and charismatic players in the history of baseball, and his name has become synonymous with his successful career and his famous quotes.

88

Joel Youngblood, a former Major League Baseball player, is known for his remarkable feat of getting hits for two different teams in the same day.

On August 4, 1982, Youngblood was a player for the New York Mets and was scheduled to play a day game against the Chicago Cubs at Wrigley Field.

During the game, Youngblood got a hit, but his day wouldn't end there.

After the game, while the Mets were traveling to their next destination, Youngblood was traded to the Montreal Expos in a trade deal.

That same night, without even having the chance to join his new team, Youngblood was inserted into the lineup for the Expos in a night game against the Philadelphia Phillies at Veterans Stadium.

In the game against the Phillies, Youngblood got another hit, thus becoming the only player in Major League Baseball history to get hits for two different teams in the same day.

It was an impressive and unique feat that earned him a place in the baseball record books.

Joel Youngblood's achievement stands out not only for the fact that he got hits for two different teams in the same day but also for the logistical and tight timing in which it occurred.

It is an uncommon milestone that showcases Youngblood's versatility and talent as a baseball player.

Joel Youngblood played in the Major Leagues for 14 seasons, primarily as an outfielder.

In addition to his notable feat of getting hits for two teams in one day, Youngblood had a solid career and contributed to several teams throughout his career.

89

The baseball cap is an iconic part of players' uniforms and has been a distinctive element of the sport for a long time.

While it is difficult to accurately trace the origins of the first straw baseball cap, it is known that the New York Knickerbockers were pioneers in the use of caps in baseball.

On April 24, 1849, the Knickerbockers, one of the early organized baseball teams, wore caps for the first time during a game.

However, at that time, these caps were likely made of materials like wool or cotton, rather than straw.

In the following years, the Knickerbockers started using fine merino wool caps with an attached crown and visor, which is considered a prototype of modern baseball caps.

These caps became one of the most popular styles and remained an essential part of players' uniforms.

Over the years, baseball caps have evolved in terms of design, materials, and details, but the general idea of a cap with a crown and visor has stayed the same.

Baseball caps have become a recognized and cherished symbol in the world of baseball, both for players and fans.

While the straw cap is not considered common in modern baseball, it may have been used in some earlier or regional contexts.

However, its use has not been upheld in the general tradition of baseball, and wool caps and other materials have become the norm in the sport.

90

The specific balk rules in baseball were not introduced until 1898.

Prior to that date, there was no clear definition of what would constitute a balk and how it would be enforced.

The introduction of balk rules in 1898 had the primary goal of preventing pitchers from intentionally deceiving baserunners.

Before this amendment, pitchers had more freedom to make deceptive movements in order to confuse or hold baserunners.

This gave an unfair advantage to pitchers and hindered the progress of runners.

The balk rules established a series of restrictions on how pitchers could make movements on the mound without delivering the ball to the plate.

These rules aim to maintain fairness and prevent pitchers from gaining an unfair advantage in the game.

Section 8 of the Major League Baseball (MLB) rules specifies the exact constitution of a balk and describes a legal pitching delivery.

According to these rules, any movement by the pitcher that is deemed deceptive or intended to hold baserunners without delivering the ball to the plate will be considered a balk.

Balk rules have contributed to a fairer game and have forced pitchers to adhere to certain protocols on the mound.

This has led to baserunners acting more conservatively and reduced the chances of pitchers gaining unfair advantages.

91

WAR (Wins Above Replacement) is a statistical metric used in baseball to assess the value of a player in all facets of the game compared to a replacement-level player.

It is a comprehensive measure that attempts to quantify a player's contribution to their team's success.

The concept of WAR is based on the idea of comparing a player's performance to the theoretical performance of an average or replacement-level player at the same position.

WAR is calculated using a complex formula that takes into account multiple statistics and variables.

WAR takes into consideration a player's different skills and contributions in baseball, such as batting, baserunning, defense, and pitching (for non-pitchers).

The position a player plays is also considered, as some positions may have a greater impact on the game than others.

The value of WAR is measured in terms of additional wins a player provides to their team compared to a replacement-level player.

For example, a player with a WAR of 4.0 is considered to have contributed approximately four more wins to their team compared to a replacement-level player.

WAR is widely used in baseball statistical analysis and is a valuable tool for comparing and evaluating player performance.

It can help determine which players have a significant impact on their team's success and make strategic decisions such as contract negotiations or trade moves.

It's important to note that the exact calculation of WAR may vary depending on the source and methodology used.

However, overall, WAR is a valuable measure for assessing the overall value of a player and their impact on the game.

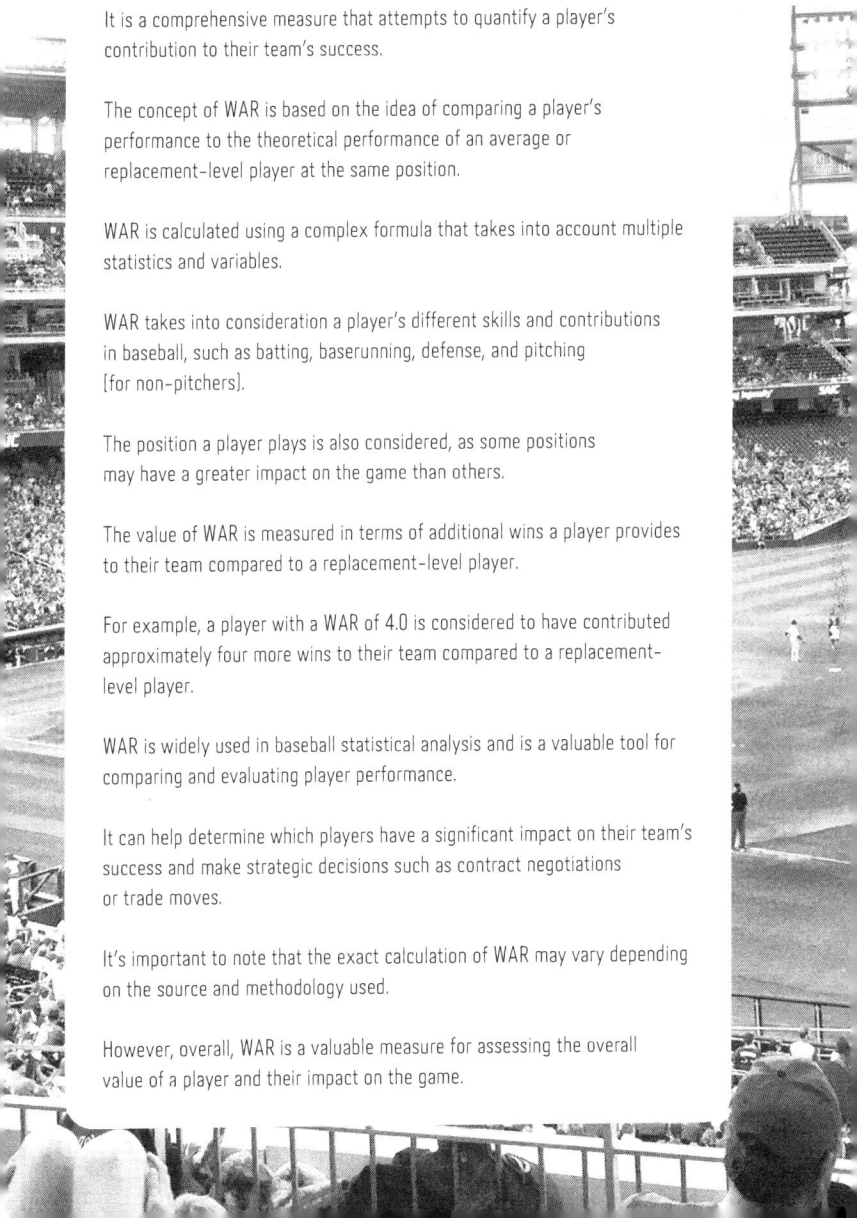

92

ERA (Earned Run Average) is a statistic used in baseball to measure a pitcher's performance.

It represents the average number of earned runs a pitcher allows per nine innings pitched.

ERA is calculated by dividing the earned runs allowed by a pitcher by the total innings pitched, and then multiplying that number by nine.

Earned runs refer to runs that score without the help of defensive errors or passed balls.

These are the runs that the pitcher is considered directly responsible for.

A low ERA indicates better performance by the pitcher, as it means they allow few earned runs compared to the number of innings pitched.

On the other hand, a high ERA indicates that the pitcher has struggled to prevent batters from scoring runs.

ERA is an important statistical tool for evaluating and comparing pitchers' performances.

It is used to determine the effectiveness and consistency of a pitcher over the course of a season or throughout their career.

It is also a key measure for ranking pitchers in leagues and for comparison between different players.

It's important to note that ERA can be influenced by external factors such as the team's defensive performance or stadium conditions.

Additionally, ERA can vary depending on the league type or the context in which the game is played, so other statistical and contextual factors should be considered when evaluating a pitcher as a whole.

93

**The wild card rule in baseball was first introduced
in 1994 in Major League Baseball (MLB).**

Prior to that date, each league (American League and National League)
consisted of two divisions, and only the winners of each division
advanced to the playoffs.

In 1994, MLB decided to expand the leagues to three divisions each, with
the goal of increasing competition and excitement in the regular season.

As a result of this expansion, the wild card rule was introduced.

This rule allowed a team with the best record that did not win its division
to have the opportunity to participate in the playoffs.

Under the wild card rule, a wild card team is added to the playoffs in each
league.

This team is selected based on its record compared to other teams that
did not win their division.

The wild card is the team with the best record that did not win its division
in each league.

The wild card team participates in a single-elimination series, usually
known as the wild card game, against another wild card-qualified team.

The winner of this game advances to the next round of the playoffs and
faces the division winner.

The introduction of the wild card rule has added additional excitement to
the playoffs and has allowed teams with good records but did not win
their division to compete for an MLB championship.

It's important to note that since its introduction in 1994, there have been
adjustments and changes in the implementation of the wild card rule in
MLB, including the addition of a second wild card game in 2012 and the
current format of a single wild card game in each league.

94

John William Lindsey, known as John Lindsey, is a professional baseball player who holds the record for spending the longest time in the minor leagues before being called up to the Major Leagues.

He was born on January 30, 1977, in Hattiesburg, Mississippi, United States.

Lindsey was selected in the 13th round of the 1995 draft by the Colorado Rockies.

He began his career in the minor leagues, playing in the Rockies' minor league system.

Over the following years, Lindsey went through several minor league organizations, including the New York Yankees, Florida Marlins, Los Angeles Dodgers, and San Diego Padres.

Despite having notable talent and performing well in the minor leagues, Lindsey did not get the opportunity to debut in the Major Leagues until the Los Angeles Dodgers called him up in 2010.

At that time, Lindsey was 33 years old.

He made his debut on May 13, 2010, against the Arizona Diamondbacks, becoming the oldest player to make his MLB debut since 1954.

Despite his late debut in the Major Leagues, Lindsey only played in seven games with the Dodgers in 2010, batting .273 with one home run and two runs batted in.

After his brief stint in the Major Leagues, Lindsey continued his career in the minor leagues and also played in foreign leagues, including Mexico.

John Lindsey's story highlights his perseverance and dedication to the game, demonstrating that it is possible to achieve the dream of playing in the Major Leagues even after spending a considerable amount of time in the minor leagues.

His record of 16 years in the minor leagues before making his Major League debut makes him an inspiring example for other players.

95

Joe McCarthy and Casey Stengel are the two coaches who share the record for the most wins in the World Series, and both established their records with the New York Yankees.

Joe McCarthy was the coach of the Yankees from 1931 to 1946.

During his tenure, McCarthy led the team to win seven World Series championships in 1932, 1936, 1937, 1938, 1939, 1941, and 1943.

Under his leadership, the Yankees had a remarkable dominance in the 1930s and early 1940s, establishing one of the most successful dynasties in baseball history.

After McCarthy, Casey Stengel took over as coach of the Yankees in 1949 and remained in the position until 1960.

During his tenure, the Yankees won seven World Series championships in 1949, 1950, 1951, 1952, 1953, 1956, and 1958.

Stengel managed to lead the team to a golden era in the 1950s, with iconic players like Mickey Mantle and Yogi Berra.

Both coaches are highly recognized in baseball history and have left a lasting legacy with the New York Yankees.

Their records of seven World Series championships with the team are a testament to their ability to guide their players to success in the most important moments of the game.

It is important to highlight that, although McCarthy and Stengel share the record for the most wins in the World Series, their legacies go beyond these individual achievements.

Both coaches are widely respected for their contribution to the game and have left an indelible mark on the history of the Yankees and baseball in general.

96

Connie Mack.

His real name was Cornelius McGillicuddy, and he was a prominent baseball coach who managed the Philadelphia Athletics from 1901 to the 1950 season.

He is widely recognized as the coach with the most victories in Major League Baseball (MLB) history.

During his time as the coach of the Athletics, Connie Mack achieved an impressive record of 3,731 wins and 3,948 losses.

His longevity in the sport and his ability to stay in the coaching position for 50 years are truly remarkable.

In addition to being a coach, Connie Mack was also the owner and general manager of the Philadelphia Athletics.

He was an influential figure in the organization and played a key role in building and sustaining the team's success.

Mack helped establish the Athletics in Philadelphia after playing for 15 years as a catcher in the Major Leagues.

In addition to his role as a coach and manager, he also held managerial positions within the team.

Throughout his career, Connie Mack won five World Series championships with the Athletics in 1910, 1911, 1913, 1929, and 1930.

His focus on building strong teams and his ability to develop talent were crucial to the Athletics' success during his tenure.

Due to his longevity in the sport and his record of victories, it is unlikely that any coach will surpass Connie Mack's record for the most wins in Major League Baseball history.

His legacy endures as one of the most influential and successful coaches in baseball history.

97

Nolan Ryan. He is widely recognized as one of the most dominant pitchers in Major League Baseball (MLB) history.

He was born on January 31, 1947, in Refugio, Texas, and became an icon of the game during his career spanning four decades.

Ryan made his debut in the Major Leagues in 1966 at the age of 19 with the New York Mets.

Throughout his career, he played for several teams, including the Mets, California Angels, Houston Astros, and Texas Rangers.

Nolan Ryan's most notable record is his all-time record for strikeouts.

He accumulated a total of 5,714 strikeouts throughout his career, surpassing all other pitchers in the history of Major League Baseball.

His ability to throw powerful pitches and his aggressive approach made him a feared pitcher by batters.

In addition to his strikeout record, Ryan also achieved other impressive milestones in his career.

He was selected to the All-Star Game eight times and won the Cy Young Award twice.

He also pitched seven no-hitters, another record in baseball history.

The longevity of Ryan's career is equally remarkable.

He retired in 1993 at the age of 46 after playing 27 seasons in the Major Leagues.

His dedication to the game, work ethic, and physical endurance allowed him to compete at a high level for such a long time.

After his retirement as a player, Nolan Ryan continued to be involved in baseball.

He became an owner and executive of teams, including the Texas Rangers, and also worked in advisory and talent development roles.

In recognition of his outstanding career, Nolan Ryan was inducted into the Baseball Hall of Fame in 1999, in his first year of eligibility.

His legacy as one of the most dominant and successful pitchers of all time continues to be admired by baseball fans and players to this day.

98

Dodger Stadium.

Located in Los Angeles, California, it is the largest baseball stadium in the United States.

It has a seating capacity of 56,000, making it the largest baseball stadium in the country.

It was opened on April 10, 1962 and serves as the home stadium for the Los Angeles Dodgers, a Major League Baseball team.

Regarding the Estadio Latinoamericano in Havana, Cuba, it is mentioned to have a seating capacity of 55,000.

However, Dodger Stadium surpasses this stadium in capacity, as it has an additional 1,000 seats.

Therefore, Dodger Stadium is considered the largest baseball stadium in the world.

As for the RingCentral Coliseum, also known as the Oakland Coliseum, it is a stadium located in Oakland, California.

It is the home stadium for the Oakland Athletics in Major League Baseball and was previously the home of the Oakland Raiders in the National Football League (NFL).

In 1996, the stadium expanded its capacity to 63,132 seats.

However, due to the current usage of the stadium, the capacity has been reduced to just over 47,000 seats.

99

The baseball team of the Arizona Diamondbacks has a unique feature in their stadium, Chase Field.

In this stadium, fans have the opportunity to enjoy the game from a pool located inside the stadium.

The pool is situated in right field of the stadium, behind the outfield fence.

To access the pool and watch the game from there, fans must purchase tickets for the stadium's pool suite.

This suite can accommodate 35 people and offers an exclusive and luxurious experience to watch baseball.

The pool suite is very popular among Diamondbacks fans, and season tickets for it usually sell out early, typically by early May.

This means that fans interested in enjoying the game from the pool must make sure to acquire their tickets in advance.

The experience of watching the game from the Chase Field pool suite offers a unique and refreshing view, as fans can enjoy the excitement of baseball while relaxing in the water.

It is a unique way to enjoy a game and one of the distinctive features of the Arizona Diamondbacks' stadium.

100

The use of illegal substances in baseball has been a controversial issue in the sport.

Some players have been involved in cheating cases related to the use of substances to enhance their performance.

-Michael Pineda: In 2014, Pineda, a Dominican pitcher who was playing for the New York Yankees at the time, was suspended for 10 games for having pine tar on his neck during a game.

Pine tar is often used by pitchers to improve grip on the ball, which is against baseball rules.

-Mark McGwire: This renowned Major League hitter has also been linked to the use of steroids.

McGwire broke the single-season home run record previously set by Roger Maris in 1998, but he has also faced controversy due to doping allegations.

In 2010, McGwire publicly admitted to using steroids during his playing career.

-Alex Rodriguez: Known as A-Rod, he is another prominent player who has been involved in doping cases.

A-Rod has been suspended twice for the use of banned substances. In 2009, he admitted to using steroids between 2001 and 2003 while playing for the Texas Rangers.

Then, in 2014, he was suspended for the entire season due to his involvement in the Biogenesis Clinic scandal, where evidence of prohibited substance use was found.

101

Throughout the history of baseball, there have been players who have earned significant sums of money through contracts, sponsorship deals, and other sports-related income.

-Alex Rodriguez: Also known as A-Rod, he is considered one of the highest-earning baseball players in his career. He signed lucrative contracts with the Texas Rangers and the New York Yankees, reaching a 10-year, $275 million agreement with the Yankees in 2007.

-Derek Jeter: The former shortstop of the New York Yankees also amassed substantial earnings during his career. Jeter was one of the most recognized and successful players of his generation and earned around $265 million in salaries throughout his career.

-Albert Pujols: He is another player who has earned considerable earnings. During his time with the St. Louis Cardinals and the Los Angeles Angels, Pujols has earned around $300 million in salaries.

-Miguel Cabrera: He is an outstanding Venezuelan hitter who has signed lucrative contracts with the Florida Marlins (now Miami Marlins) and the Detroit Tigers. Cabrera has earned around $320 million in salaries throughout his career.

-Clayton Kershaw: He is one of the standout pitchers for the Los Angeles Dodgers and has secured lucrative contracts. In 2014, he signed a seven-year, $215 million contract with the Dodgers.

If you have found the fascinating trivia we've gathered about the exciting world of baseball interesting, we would like to ask you to leave us a review on Amazon.

Your perspective is immensely valuable, not only to us but also to those baseball enthusiasts looking to enrich their knowledge and delight in new facts.

We understand that writing a review may seem like a somewhat laborious process, but we kindly ask that you set aside a few minutes of your time to share your impressions and ratings with us.

Your support is greatly appreciated, as it motivates us to continue producing high-quality content for all fans of this thrilling sport.

We extend our heartfelt thanks for your endorsement and sincerely hope that you have enjoyed immersing yourself in the pages of our book as much as we enjoyed creating it.

We deeply appreciate you sharing your experience with us!

⭐ ⭐ ⭐ ⭐ ⭐

Printed in Great Britain
by Amazon